LET'S LEARN

מִילוֹן תְּמוּנוֹת עִבְרִי-אַנְגְלִי

HEBREW PICTURE DICTIONARY

By
The Editors of
Passport Books

Illustrated by
Marlene Goodman

PASSPORT BOOKS
NTC/Contemporary Publishing Group

Welcome to the *Let's Learn Hebrew* Picture Dictionary!

Here's an exciting way for you to learn more than 1,500 words that will help you speak about many of your favorite subjects. With these words, you will be able to talk about your house, sports, outer space, the ocean, and many more subjects.

This dictionary is fun to use. On each page, you will see drawings with the words that describe them underneath. These drawings are usually part of a large, colorful scene. See if you can find all the words in the big scene! You will enjoy looking at the pictures more and more as you learn new words.

At the back of the book, you will find a Hebrew-English Glossary and Index and an English-Hebrew Glossary and Index, where you can look up words in alphabetical order, and find out exactly where the words are located in the dictionary.

This is a book you can look at over and over again, and each time you look, you will find something new. You'll be able to talk about people, places, and things you know, and you'll learn lots of new words as you go along!

Library of Congress Cataloging-in-Publication Data
is available from the United States Library of Congress.

Illustrations by Terrie Meider
7. Clothing; 15. People in our Community; 18. Sports; 28. Colors;
29. The Family Tree; 30. Shapes; 31. Numbers; 32. Map of the World.

Published by Passport Books
An imprint of NTC/Contemporary Publishing Company

International Standard Book Number: 0-8442-8490-4

1 2 3 4 5 6 7 8 9 RRW 05 04 03 02

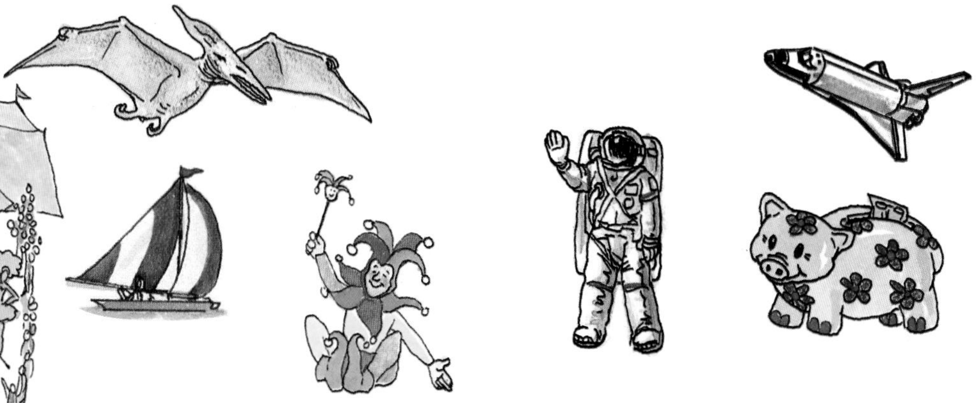

Table of Contents *toĥen ha'inyanim* תּוֹכֶן הָעִנְיָנִים

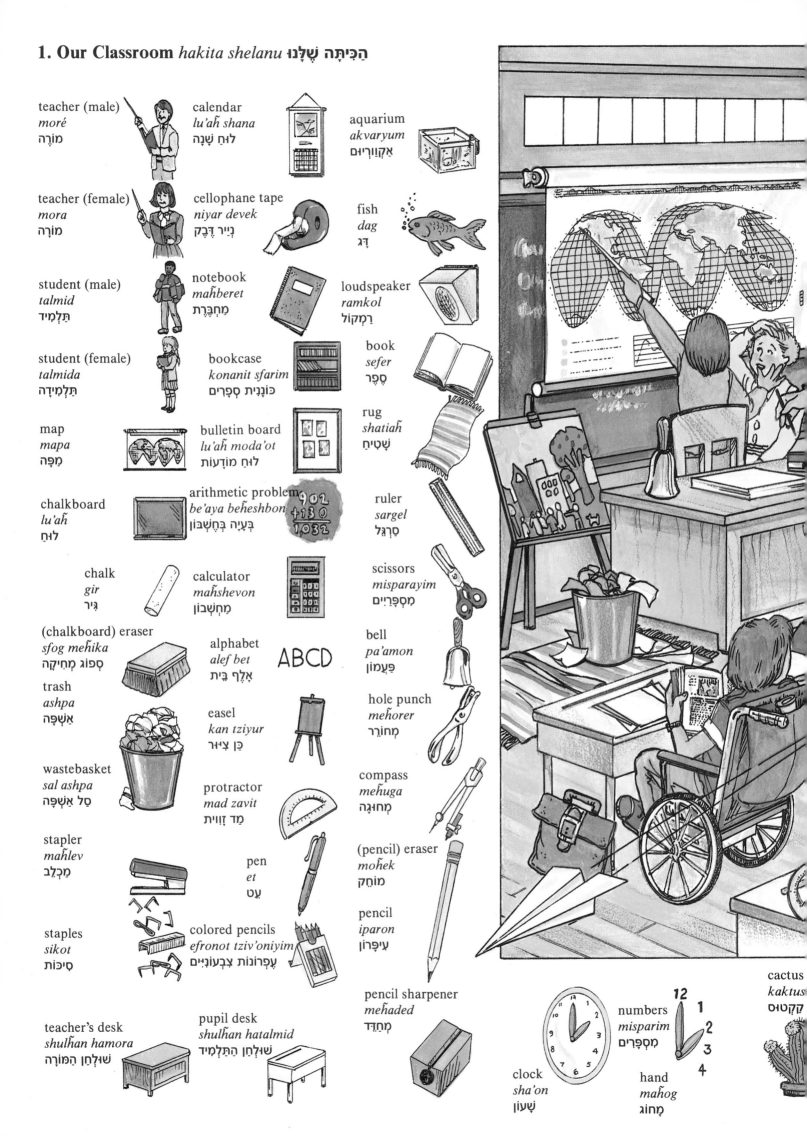

1. Our Classroom *hakita shelanu* הַכִּיתָּה שֶׁלָּנוּ

teacher (male) — *moré* — מוֹרֶה

teacher (female) — *mora* — מוֹרָה

student (male) — *talmid* — תַּלְמִיד

student (female) — *talmida* — תַּלְמִידָה

map — *mapa* — מַפָּה

chalkboard — *lu'ah̃* — לוּחַ

chalk — *gir* — גִּיר

(chalkboard) eraser — *sfog meh̃ika* — סְפוֹג מְחִיקָה

trash — *ashpa* — אַשְׁפָּה

wastebasket — *sal ashpa* — סַל אַשְׁפָּה

stapler — *mah̃lev* — מַכְלֵב

staples — *sikot* — סִיכּוֹת

teacher's desk — *shulh̃an hamora* — שׁוּלְחַן הַמּוֹרֶה

calendar — *lu'ah̃ shana* — לוּחַ שָׁנָה

cellophane tape — *niyar devek* — נְיַיר דֶּבֶק

notebook — *mah̃beret* — מַחְבֶּרֶת

bookcase — *konanit sfarim* — כּוֹנָנִית סְפָרִים

bulletin board — *lu'ah̃ moda'ot* — לוּחַ מוֹדָעוֹת

arithmetic problem — *be'aya beh̃eshbon* — בְּעָיָה בְּחֶשְׁבּוֹן

902
+130
1032

calculator — *mah̃shevon* — מַחְשֵׁבוֹן

alphabet — *alef bet* — אָלֶף בֵּית

ABCD

easel — *kan tziyur* — כַּן צִיּוּר

protractor — *mad zavit* — מַד זָווִית

pen — *et* — עֵט

colored pencils — *efronot tziv'oniyim* — עֶפְרוֹנוֹת צִבְעוֹנִיִּים

pupil desk — *shulh̃an hatalmid* — שׁוּלְחַן הַתַּלְמִיד

aquarium — *akvaryum* — אַקְוַורְיוּם

fish — *dag* — דָּג

loudspeaker — *ramkol* — רַמְקוֹל

book — *sefer* — סֵפֶר

rug — *shatiah̃* — שָׁטִיחַ

ruler — *sargel* — סַרְגֵּל

scissors — *misparayim* — מִסְפָּרַיִים

bell — *pa'amon* — פַּעֲמוֹן

hole punch — *meh̃orer* — מְחוֹרֵר

compass — *meh̃uga* — מְחוּגָה

(pencil) eraser — *moh̃ek* — מוֹחֵק

pencil — *iparon* — עִיפָּרוֹן

pencil sharpener — *meh̃aded* — מְחַדֵּד

clock — *sha'on* — שָׁעוֹן

numbers — *misparim* — מִסְפָּרִים

12 1 2 3 4

hand — *mah̃og* — מָחוֹג

cactus — *kaktus* — קַקְטוּס

plant
tzemaĥ
צֶמַח
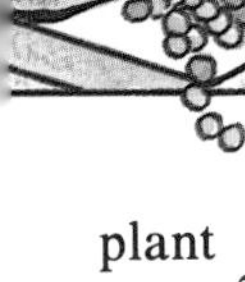

glue
devek
דֶּבֶק

globe
globus
גְּלוֹבּוּס

picture
tmuna
תְּמוּנָה

paint
tzeva
צֶבַע
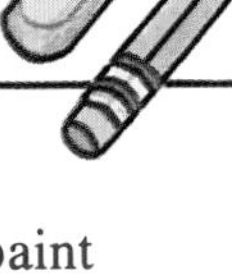

paintbrush
miĥol
מִכְחוֹל

paper
niyar
נְיָיר

crayon
tzeva
צֶבַע

2. Our House *habayit shelanu* הַבַּיִת שֶׁלָּנוּ

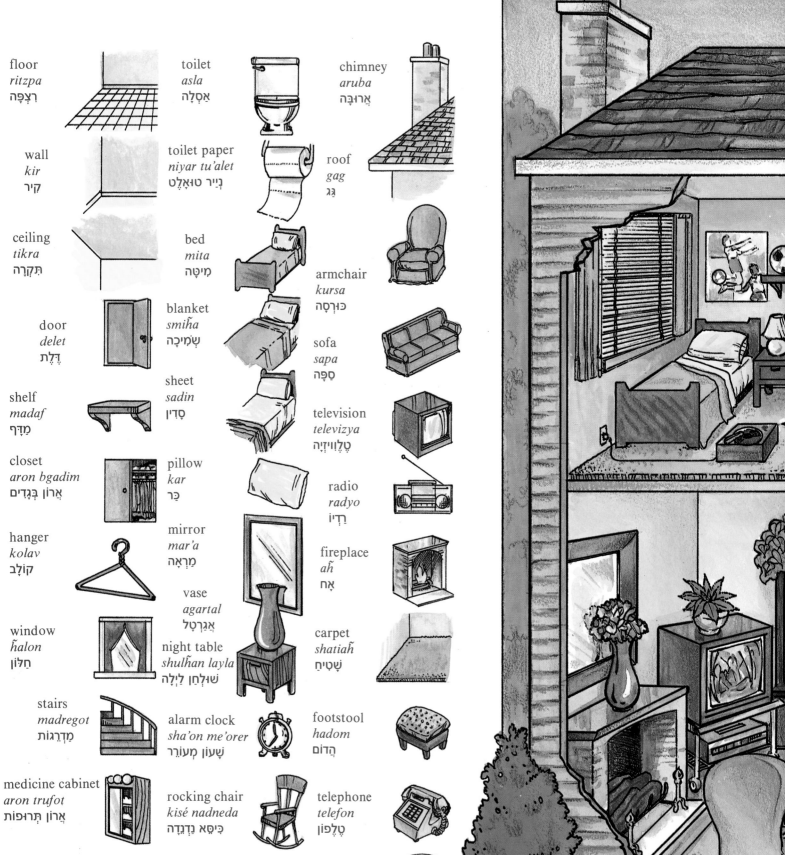

floor
ritzpa
רִצְפָּה

wall
kir
קִיר

ceiling
tikra
תִּקְרָה

door
delet
דֶּלֶת

shelf
madaf
מַדָּף

closet
aron bgadim
אֲרוֹן בְּגָדִים

hanger
kolav
קוֹלָב

window
ḣalon
חַלּוֹן

stairs
madregot
מַדְרֵגוֹת

medicine cabinet
aron trufot
אֲרוֹן תְּרוּפוֹת

bathtub
ambatya
אַמְבַּטְיָה

shower
miklaḣat
מִקְלַחַת

towel
magevet
מַגֶּבֶת

toilet
asla
אַסְלָה

toilet paper
niyar tu'alet
נְיַר טוּאָלֶט

bed
mita
מִיטָּה

blanket
smiḣa
שְׂמִיכָה

sheet
sadin
סָדִין

pillow
kar
כַּר

mirror
mar'a
מַרְאָה

vase
agartal
אֲגַרְטָל

night table
shulḣan layla
שׁוּלְחַן לַיְלָה

alarm clock
sha'on me'orer
שְׁעוֹן מְעוֹרֵר

rocking chair
kisé nadneda
כִּיסֵּא נַדְנֵדָה

curtains
vilon
וִילוֹן

venetian blinds
tris rafafot
תְּרִיס רְפָפוֹת

poster
poster
פּוֹסְטֶר

chimney
aruba
אֲרוּבָּה

roof
gag
גַּג

armchair
kursa
כּוּרְסָה

sofa
sapa
סַפָּה

television
televizya
טֶלֶוִויזְיָה

radio
radyo
רַדְיוֹ

fireplace
aḣ
אָח

carpet
shatiaḣ
שָׁטִיחַ

footstool
hadom
הֲדוֹם

telephone
telefon
טֶלֶפוֹן

lamp
menora
מְנוֹרָה

dresser
shida
שִׁידָּה

record
taklit
תַּקְלִיט

record player
patéfon
פָּטֵיפוֹן

compact disc
taklitor
תַּקְלִיטוֹר

videocassette player
maḣshir vidyo
מַכְשִׁיר וִידֵאוֹ

cassette tape
kaletet
קַלֶּטֶת

cassette player
reshamkol
רְשַׁמְקוֹל

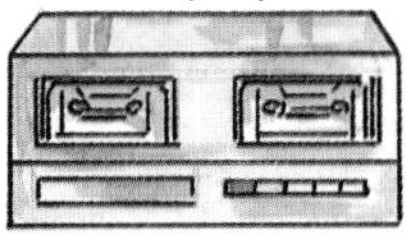

bedroom
h̃adar sheyna
חֲדַר שֵׁינָה

bathroom
h̃adar ambatya
חֲדַר אַמְבַּטְיָה

living room
h̃adar megurim
חֲדַר מְגוּרִים

dining room
h̃adar oh̃el
חֲדַר אוֹכֶל

kitchen
mitbah̃
מִטְבָּח

3. The Kitchen *hamitbaĥ* הַמִּטְבָּח

counter
delpek
דֶּלְפֵּק

oven
tanur afiya
תַּנּוּר אֲפִיָּה

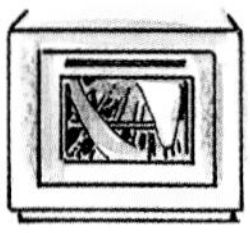

faucet
berez
בֶּרֶז

pan
maĥavat
מַחֲבַת

paper towels
magvot niyar
מַגָּבוֹת נְיָר

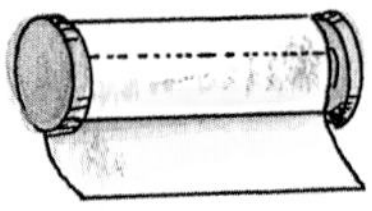

chair
kisé
כִּסֵּא

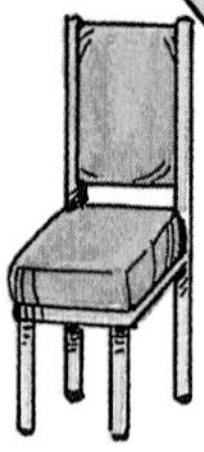

table
shulĥan
שֻׁלְחָן

refrigerator
mekarer
מְקָרֵר

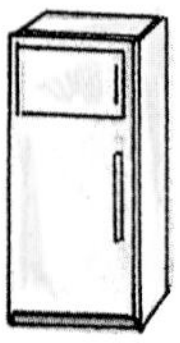

dishwasher
mediaĥ kelim
מֵדִיחַ כֵּלִים

electric mixer
me'arbel ĥashmali
מְעַרְבֵּל חַשְׁמַלִּי

ice cubes
kubiyot keraĥ
קוּבִּיּוֹת קֶרַח

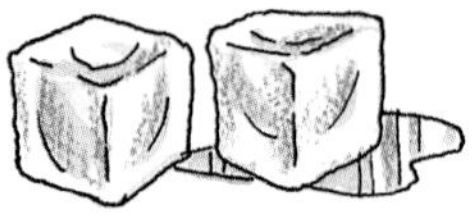

apron
sinor
סִינּוֹר

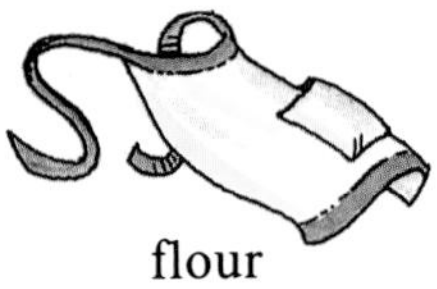

microwave oven
tanur mikrogal
תַּנּוּר מִיקְרוֹגָל

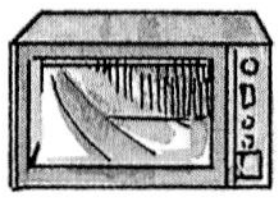

freezer
ta hakpa'a
תָּא הַקְפָּאָה

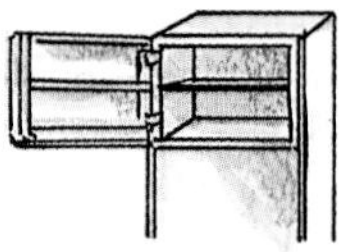

food processor
me'abed mazon
מְעַבֵּד מָזוֹן

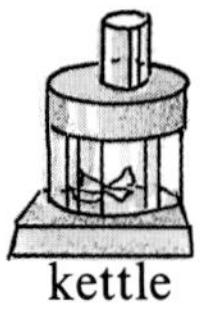

drawer
megera
מְגֵרָה

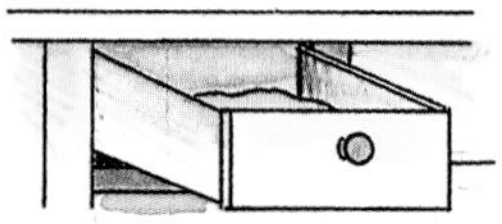

spatula
marit
מָרִית

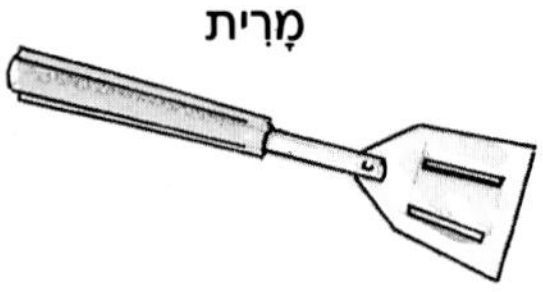

flour
kemaĥ
קֶמַח

stove
kirayim
כִּירַיִם

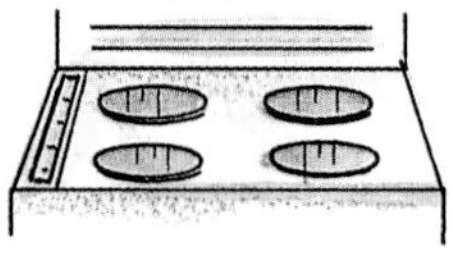

sink
kiyor
כִּיּוֹר

kettle
kumkum
קוּמְקוּם

toaster
matznem
מַצְנֵם

dishes
kelim
כֵּלִים

sponge
sfog
סְפוֹג

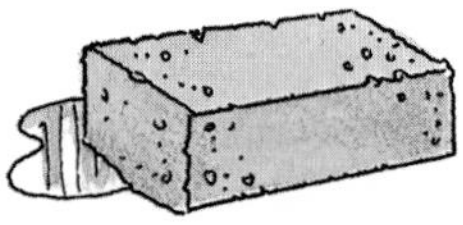

The Utility Room *ĥadar hasherut* חֲדַר הַשֵּׁירוּת

washing machine
meĥonat kvisa
מְכוֹנַת כְּבִיסָה

iron
maghetz
מַגְהֵץ

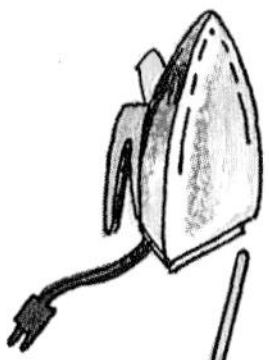

screw
boreg
בּוֹרֶג

toolbox
argaz kelim
אַרְגַּז כֵּלִים

laundry detergent
avkat kvisa
אַבְקַת כְּבִיסָה

laundry
kvisa
כְּבִיסָה

broom
mataté
מַטְאֲטֵא

mop
sĥava al makel
סְחָבָה עַל מַקֵּל

screwdriver
mavreg
מַבְרֵג

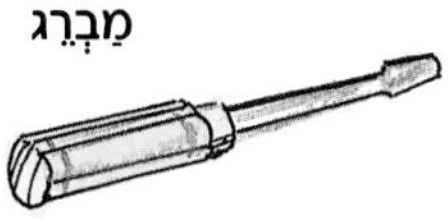

wrench
mafte'aĥ bragim
מַפְתֵּחַ בְּרָגִים

wood
etz
עֵץ

board
keresh
קֶרֶשׁ

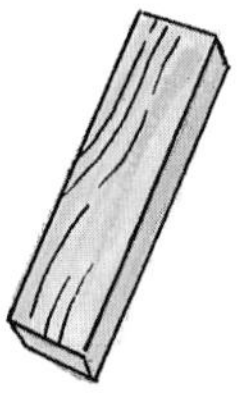

dustpan
ya'é
יָעֶה

electrical outlet
sheka ĥashmali
שֶׁקַע חַשְׁמַלִּי

cuum cleaner
'ev avak
שׁוֹאֵב אָ

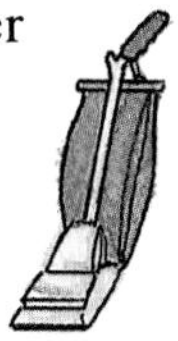

drill
makdeĥa
מַקְדֵּחָה

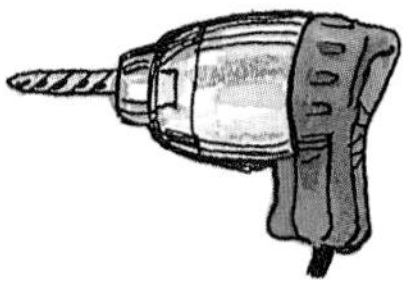

sandpaper
niyar letesh
נְיַר לֶטֶשׁ

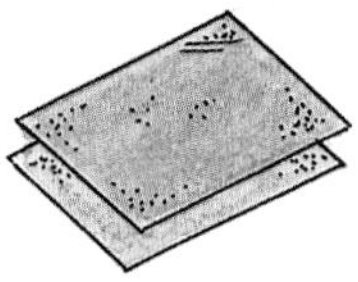

flashlight
panas
פָּנָס

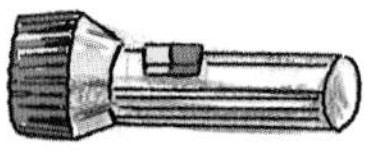

brick
levena
לְבֵנָה

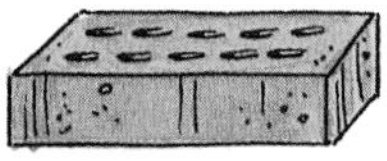

hammer
patish
פַּטִּישׁ

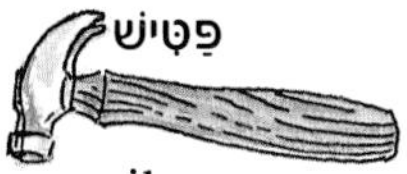

ironing board
lu'aĥ gihutz
לוּחַ גִּיהוּץ

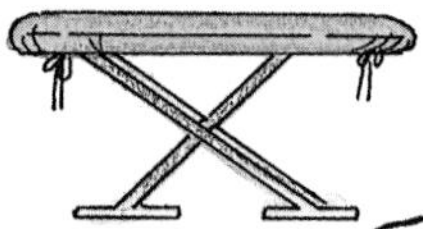

nail
masmer
מַסְמֵר

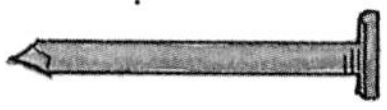

file
ptzira
פְּצִירָה

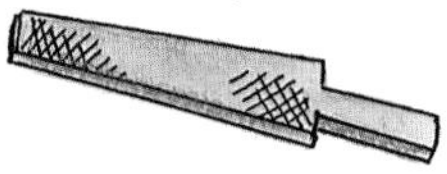

tape measure
meter
מֶטֶר

saw
masor
מַסּוֹר

clothes dryer
meyabesh kvisa
מְיַיבֵּשׁ כְּבִיסָה

4. The Attic *aliyat hagag* עֲלִיַּית הַגָּג

trunk
argaz
אַרְגָּז

box
kufsa
קוּפְסָה

dust
avak
אָבָק

string
ĥut
חוּט

cobweb
kurey akavish
קוּרֵי עַכָּבִישׁ

ball gown
simlat neshef
שִׂמְלַת נֶשֶׁף

top hat
tzilinder
צִילִינְדֶר

tuxedo
toksido
טוֹקְסִידוֹ

hat
kova
כּוֹבַע

feather
notza
נוֹצָה

cowboy hat
kova bokrim
כּוֹבַע בּוֹקְרִים

uniform
madim
מַדִּים

cowboy boots
magfey bokrim
מַגְפֵי בּוֹקְרִים

photo album
albom tmunot
אַלְבּוֹם תְּמוּנוֹת

game
misĥak
מִשְׂחָק

doll
buba
בּוּבָּה

jigsaw puzzle
pazel
פָּאזֶל

jump rope
dalgit
דַּלְגִית

teddy bear
dubi
דּוּבִּי

toys
tza'atzu'im
צַעֲצוּעִים

whistle
mashrokit
מַשְׁרוֹקִית

cards
klafim
קְלָפִים

dice
kubiyot
קוּבִּיּוֹת

blocks
kubiyot
קוּבִּיּוֹת

electric train
rakevet ĥashmalit
רַכֶּבֶת חַשְׁמַלִּית

magnet
magnet
מַגְנֵט

cradle
arisa
עֲרִיסָה

coloring book
ĥoveret tzvi'a
חוֹבֶרֶת צְבִיעָה

music box
teyvat negina
תֵּיבַת נְגִינָה

yarn
ĥut
חוּט

knitting needles
masrégot
מַסְרֵגוֹת

dollhouse
beyt bubot
בֵּית בּוּבּוֹת

comic books
ĥovrot metzuyarot
חוֹבְרוֹת מְצוּיָּרוֹת

lightbulb
nura
נוּרָה

toy soldiers
ĥayaley tza'atzu'a
חַיָּילֵי צַעֲצוּעַ

movie projector
makrena
מַקְרֵנָה

umbrella
mitriya
מִטְרִיָּה

puppet
buba
בּוּבָּה

fan
menifa
מְנִיפָה

marbles
gulot
גּוּלוֹת

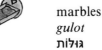

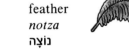

rocking horse
sus nadneda
סוּס נַדְנֵדָה

chess
shaĥmat
שַׁחְמָט

photograph
tatzlum
תַּצְלוּם

spinning wheel
galgal tviya
גַּלְגַּל טְווִיָּה

picture frame
misgeret
מִסְגֶּרֶת

rocking chair
kisé nadneda
כִּסֵּא נַדְנֵדָה

checkers
damka
דַּמְקָה

5. The Four Seasons (Weather) *arba ha'onot (mezeg ha'avir)* אַרְבַּע הָעוֹנוֹת (מֶזֶג הָאֲוִויר)

Winter
ĥoref
חוֹרֶף

snow
sheleg
שֶׁלֶג
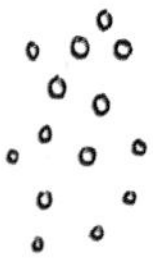

sled
mizĥelet
מִזְחֶלֶת

ice
keraĥ
קֶרַח

snowplow
mefaleset sheleg
מְפַלֶּסֶת שֶׁלֶג

snowflake
ptot sheleg
פְּתוֹת שֶׁלֶג

snowmobile
ofano'a sheleg
אוֹפַנּוֹעַ שֶׁלֶג

icicle
netif keraĥ
נְטִיף קֶרַח

snowman
ish sheleg
אִישׁ שֶׁלֶג

shovel
et
אֵת

snowball
kadur sheleg
כַּדּוּר שֶׁלֶג

snowstorm
sufat sheleg
סוּפַת שֶׁלֶג

log
bul etz
בּוּל עֵץ

Spring
aviv
אָבִיב

rain
geshem
גֶּשֶׁם

flowers
praĥim
פְּרָחִים

rainbow
keshet
קֶשֶׁת

flowerbed
aruga
עֲרוּגָה

stem
giv'ol
גִּבְעוֹל

petal
alé koteret
עֲלֵה כּוֹתֶרֶת

bird
tzipor
צִיפּוֹר

vegetable garden
gan yarak
גַּן יָרָק

worm
tola'at
תּוֹלַעַת

raindrop
tipat geshem
טִיפַּת גֶּשֶׁם

lightning
barak
בָּרָק

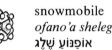

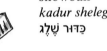

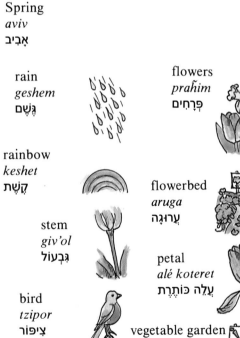

Summer
ka'yitz
קַיִץ

butterfly
parpar
פַּרְפַּר

fly
zvuv
זְבוּב

fly swatter
maȟbet zvuvim
מַחְבֵּט זְבוּבִים

fan
me'avrer
מְאַוְרֵר

sprinkler
mamtera
מַמְטֵרָה

grasshopper
ȟagav
חָגָב

lawn mower
maȟseȟat deshé
מַכְסֵחַת דֶּשֶׁא

barbecue
askala
אַסְכָּלָה

hammock
arsal
עַרְסָל

yard
ȟatzer
חָצֵר

deck
mirpeset
מִרְפֶּסֶת

garden hose
tzinor hashkaya
צִינּוֹר הַשְׁקָיָה

matches
gafrurim
גַּפְרוּרִים

Fall
stav
סְתָיו

wind
ru'aȟ
רוּחַ

leaf
alé
עָלֶה

branch
anaf
עָנָף

fog
arafel
עֲרָפֶל

rake
magrefa
מַגְרֵפָה

clouds
ananim
עֲנָנִים

kite
afifon
עֲפִיפוֹן

puddle
shlulit
שְׁלוּלִית

mud
botz
בּוֹץ
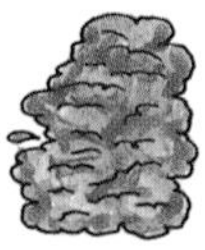

bird's nest
ken shel tzipor
קֵן שֶׁל צִיפּוֹר

bush
si'aȟ
שִׂיחַ
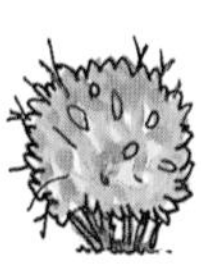

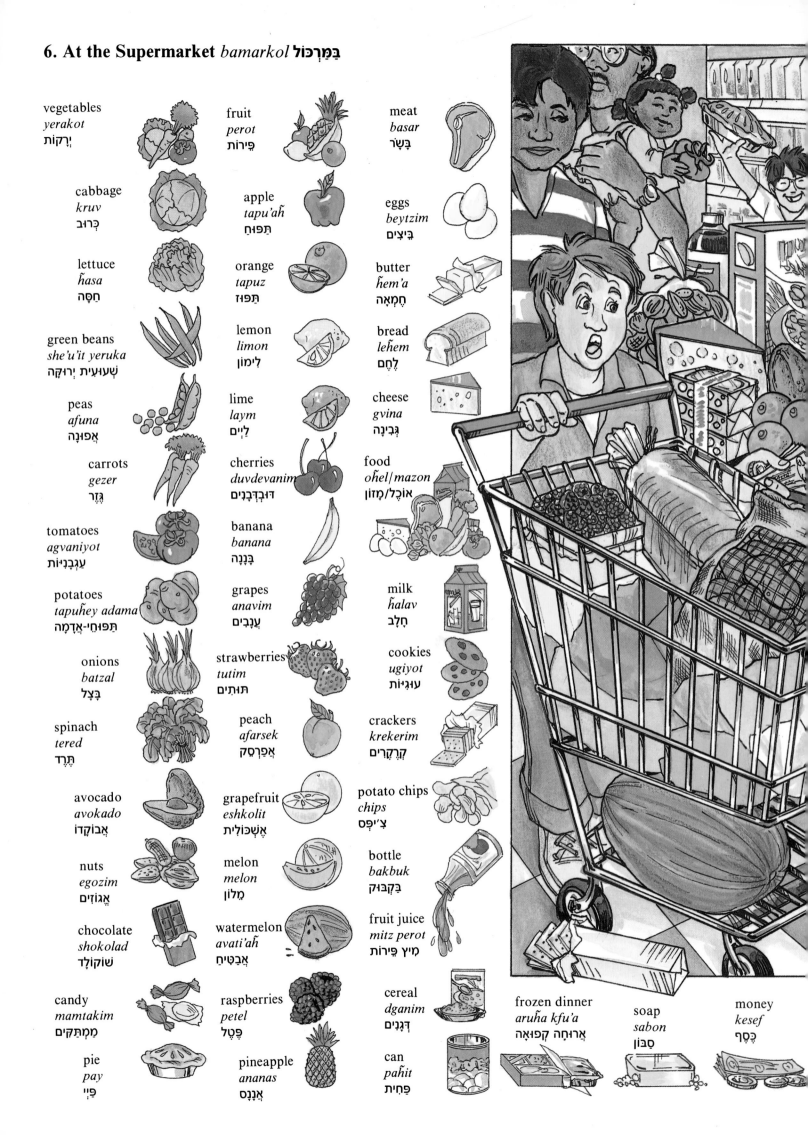

6. At the Supermarket *bamarkol* בַּמַּרְכּוֹל

vegetables
yerakot
יְרָקוֹת

cabbage
kruv
כְּרוּב

lettuce
ħasa
חַסָּה

green beans
she'u'it yeruka
שְׁעוּעִית יְרוּקָּה

peas
afuna
אֲפוּנָה

carrots
gezer
גֶּזֶר

tomatoes
agvaniyot
עַגְבָנִיּוֹת

potatoes
tapuħey adama
תַּפּוּחֵי-אֲדָמָה

onions
batzal
בָּצָל

spinach
tered
תֶּרֶד

avocado
avokado
אֲבוֹקָדוֹ

nuts
egozim
אֱגוֹזִים

chocolate
shokolad
שׁוֹקוֹלָד

candy
mamtakim
מַמְתַּקִּים

pie
pay
פַּיי

fruit
perot
פֵּירוֹת

apple
tapu'aħ
תַּפּוּחַ

orange
tapuz
תַּפּוּז

lemon
limon
לִימוֹן

lime
laym
לַיְים

cherries
duvdevanim
דּוּבְדְּבָנִים

banana
banana
בָּנָנָה

grapes
anavim
עֲנָבִים

strawberries
tutim
תּוּתִים

peach
afarsek
אֲפַרְסֵק

grapefruit
eshkolit
אֶשְׁכּוֹלִית

melon
melon
מֶלוֹן

watermelon
avati'aħ
אֲבַטִּיחַ

raspberries
petel
פֶּטֶל

pineapple
ananas
אֲנָנָס

meat
basar
בָּשָׂר

eggs
beytzim
בֵּיצִים

butter
ħem'a
חֶמְאָה

bread
leħem
לֶחֶם

cheese
gvina
גְּבִינָה

food
oħel/mazon
אוֹכֶל/מָזוֹן

milk
ħalav
חָלָב

cookies
ugiyot
עוּגִיּוֹת

crackers
krekerim
קְרֶקֶרִים

potato chips
chips
צִ׳יפְּס

bottle
bakbuk
בַּקְבּוּק

fruit juice
mitz perot
מִיץ פֵּירוֹת

cereal
dganim
דְּגָנִים

can
paħit
פַּחִית

frozen dinner
aruħa kfu'a
אֲרוּחָה קְפוּאָה

soap
sabon
סַבּוֹן

money
kesef
כֶּסֶף

hopping cart
glat kniyot
עֶגְלַת קְנִיּוֹ

shopping bag
sakit
שַׂקִּית

sign
shelet
שֶׁלֶט

scale
mozna'yim
מֹאזְנַיִם

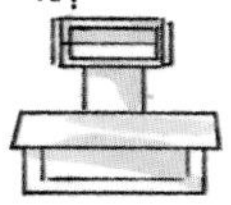

price
meħir
מְחִיר

cash register
kupa roshemet
קוּפָּה רוֹשֶׁמֶת

cashier
kupa'it
קוּפָּאִית

7. Clothing *levush* לְבוּשׁ

glasses
mishkafa'yim
מִשְׁקָפַיִים
buckle
avzem
אַבְזֵם
belt
ĥagora
חֲגוֹרָה
pants
miĥnasa'yim
מִכְנָסַיִים
collar
tzavaron
צַוָּארוֹן
blouse
kutonet
כּוּתּוֹנֶת
bracelet
tzamid
צָמִיד
ring
taba'at
טַבַּעַת
skirt
ĥatza'it
חֲצָאִית
socks
garba'yim
גַּרְבַּיִים
shoes
na'ala'yim
נַעֲלַיִים
underwear
levanim/taĥtonim
לְבָנִים/תַּחְתּוֹנִים
tie
aniva
עֲנִיבָה
necklace
sharsheret
שַׁרְשֶׁרֶת
sleeve
sharvul
שַׁרְווּל
dress
simla
שִׂמְלָה
suit
ĥalifa
חֲלִיפָה
shirt
ĥultza
חוּלְצָה
button
kaftor
כַּפְתּוֹר
bathing suit
beged yam
בֶּגֶד יָם
earmuffs
meĥamemey ozna'yim
מְחַמְּמֵי אוֹזְנַיִים
gloves
kfafot
כְּפָפוֹת
sweater
sveder
סְוֶודֶר
shoelace
sroĥ na'al
שְׂרוֹךְ נַעַל
gym shoes
na'aley hit'amlut
נַעֲלֵי הִתְעַמְּלוּת
coat
me'il
מְעִיל
handkerchief
mitpaĥat
מִטְפַּחַת
tights
garbiyonim
גַּרְבִּיּוֹנִים

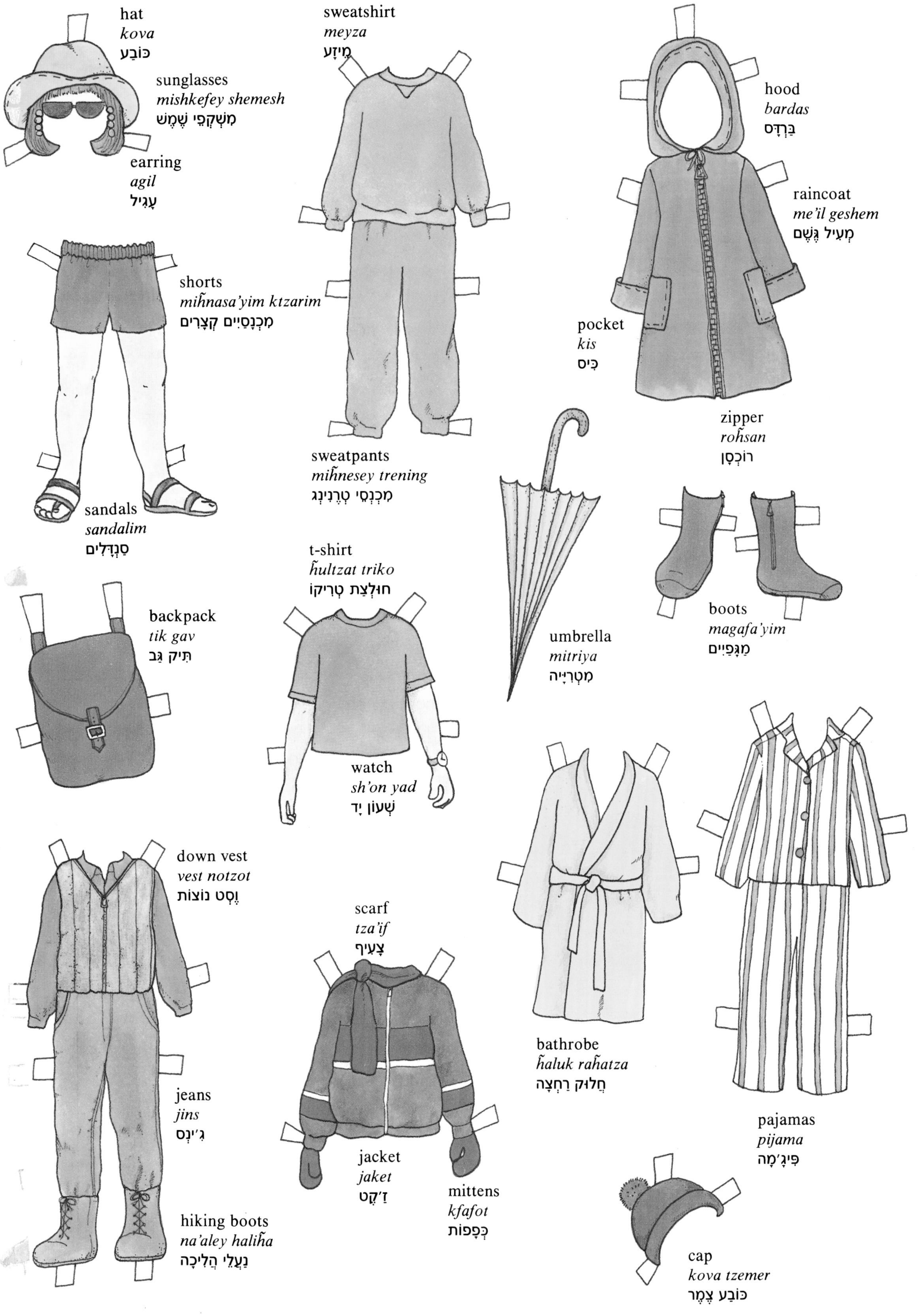
hat
kova
כּוֹבַע
sunglasses
mishkefey shemesh
מִשְׁקְפֵי שֶׁמֶשׁ
earring
agil
עָגִיל
sweatshirt
meyza
מֵיזָע
hood
bardas
בַּרְדָּס
raincoat
me'il geshem
מְעִיל גֶּשֶׁם
shorts
miȟnasa'yim ktzarim
מִכְנָסַיִים קְצָרִים
pocket
kis
כִּיס
sweatpants
miȟnesey trening
מִכְנְסֵי טְרֶנִינְג
zipper
roȟsan
רוֹכְסָן
sandals
sandalim
סַנְדָּלִים
t-shirt
ȟultzat triko
חוּלְצַת טְרִיקוֹ
boots
magafa'yim
מַגָּפַיִים
backpack
tik gav
תִּיק גַּב
umbrella
mitriya
מִטְרִיָּה
watch
sh'on yad
שְׁעוֹן יָד
down vest
vest notzot
וֶסְט נוֹצוֹת
scarf
tza'if
צָעִיף
bathrobe
ȟaluk raȟatza
חֲלוּק רַחְצָה
pajamas
pijama
פִּיגָ'מָה
jeans
jins
ג'ִינְס
jacket
jaket
זִ'קֶט
mittens
kfafot
כְּפָפוֹת
hiking boots
na'aley haliȟa
נַעֲלֵי הֲלִיכָה
cap
kova tzemer
כּוֹבַע צֶמֶר

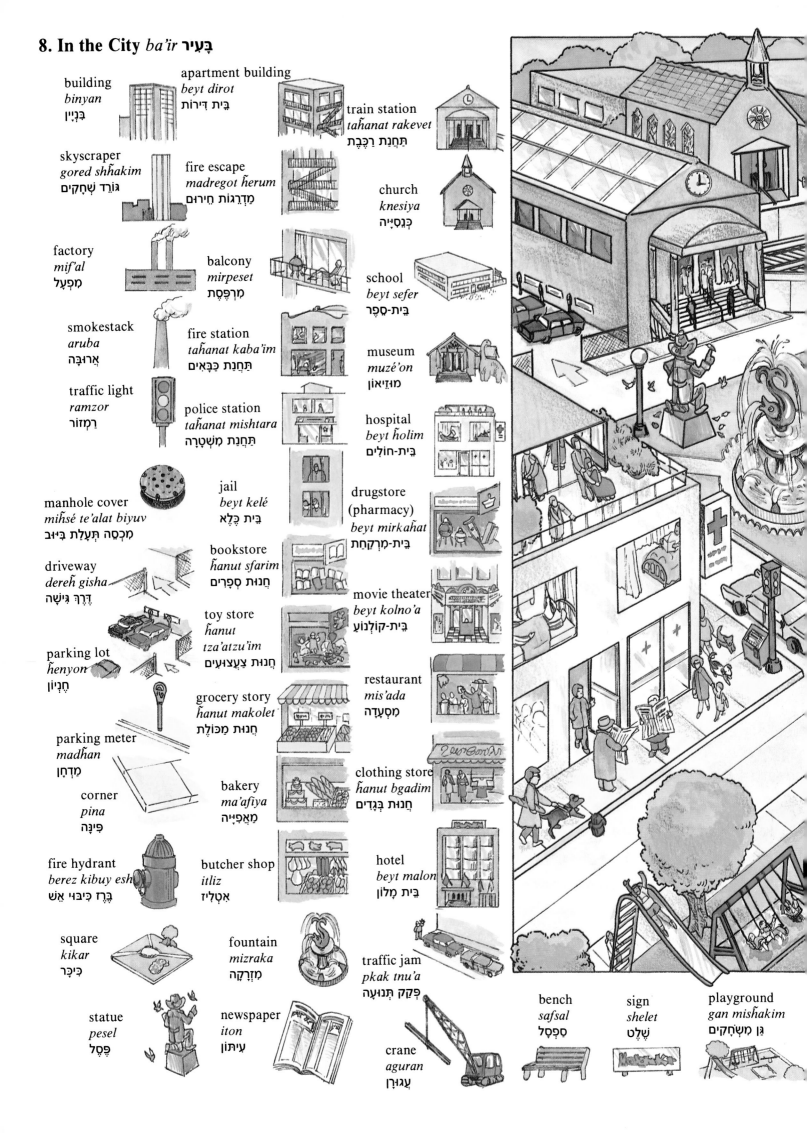

8. In the City *ba'ir* בָּעִיר

building
binyan
בִּנְיָן

skyscraper
gored shĥakim
גּוֹרֵד שְׁחָקִים

factory
mif'al
מִפְעָל

smokestack
aruba
אֲרוּבָּה

traffic light
ramzor
רַמְזוֹר

manhole cover
miĥsé te'alat biyuv
מִכְסֵה תְּעָלַת בִּיּוּב

driveway
dereĥ gisha
דֶּרֶךְ גִּישָׁה

parking lot
ĥenyon
חֶנְיוֹן

parking meter
madĥan
מַדְחָן

corner
pina
פִּינָּה

fire hydrant
berez kibuy esh
בֶּרֶז כִּיבּוּי אֵשׁ

square
kikar
כִּיכָּר

statue
pesel
פֶּסֶל

apartment building
beyt dirot
בֵּית דִּירוֹת

fire escape
madregot ĥerum
מַדְרֵגוֹת חֵירוּם

balcony
mirpeset
מִרְפֶּסֶת

fire station
taĥanat kaba'im
תַּחֲנַת כַּבָּאִים

police station
taĥanat mishtara
תַּחֲנַת מִשְׁטָרָה

jail
beyt kelé
בֵּית כֶּלֶא

bookstore
ĥanut sfarim
חֲנוּת סְפָרִים

toy store
ĥanut tza'atzu'im
חֲנוּת צַעֲצוּעִים

grocery story
ĥanut makolet
חֲנוּת מַכּוֹלֶת

bakery
ma'afiya
מַאֲפִיָּיה

butcher shop
itliz
אִטְלִיז

fountain
mizraka
מִזְרָקָה

newspaper
iton
עִיתּוֹן

train station
taĥanat rakevet
תַּחֲנַת רַכֶּבֶת

church
knesiya
כְּנֵסִיָּיה

school
beyt sefer
בֵּית-סֵפֶר

museum
muzé'on
מוּזֵיאוֹן

hospital
beyt ĥolim
בֵּית-חוֹלִים

drugstore
(pharmacy)
beyt mirkaĥat
בֵּית-מִרְקַחַת

movie theater
beyt kolno'a
בֵּית-קוֹלְנוֹעַ

restaurant
mis'ada
מִסְעָדָה

clothing store
ĥanut bgadim
חֲנוּת בְּגָדִים

hotel
beyt malon
בֵּית מָלוֹן

traffic jam
pkak tnu'a
פְּקַק תְּנוּעָה

crane
aguran
עֲגוּרָן

bench
safsal
סַפְסָל

sign
shelet
שֶׁלֶט

playground
gan mishĥakim
גַּן מִשְׂחָקִים

park
gan
גַּן

jungle gym
sulamot
סוּלָמוֹת

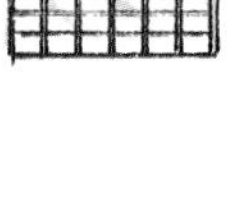

swings
nadnedot
נַדְנֵדוֹת

seesaw
alé vared
עֲלֵה וָרֵד

slide
maglesha
מַגְלֵשָׁה

sandbox
argaz ȟol
אַרְגַּז חוֹל

beach
ȟof
חוֹף

9. In the Country *bakfar* בַּכְּפָר

farmer
ikar
אִיכָּר

tractor
traktor
טְרַקְטוֹר

barn
asam
אָסָם

hay
shaĥat
שַׁחַת

dog
kelev
כֶּלֶב

puppy
klavlav
כְּלַבְלָב

cat
ĥatul
חָתוּל

kitten
ĥataltul
חֲתַלְתּוּל

rooster
tarnegol
תַּרְנְגוֹל

hen
tarnegolet
תַּרְנְגוֹלֶת

chick
efro'aĥ
אֶפְרוֹחַ

pig
ĥazir
חֲזִיר

piglet
ĥaziron
חֲזִירוֹן

rabbit
arnav
אַרְנָב

bull
par
פַּר

cow
para
פָּרָה

calf
egel
עֵגֶל

horse
sus
סוּס

colt
syaĥ
סְיָיח

duck
barvaz
בַּרְוָוז

duckling
barvazon
בַּרְווזוֹן

goat
ta'yish
תַּיִשׁ

kid
gdi
גְּדִי

goose
avaz
אַוָּוז

gosling
avazon
אַוָּוזוֹן

sheep
kivsa
כִּבְשָׂה

lamb
talé
טָלֶה

mouse
aĥbar
עַכְבָּר

horns
karna'yim
קַרְנַיִים

donkey
ĥamor
חֲמוֹר

bees
dvorim
דְּבוֹרִים

frog
tzfardé'a
צְפַרְדֵּעַ

pond
breĥa
בְּרֵכָה

grass
deshé
דֶּשֶׁא

fence
gader
גָּדֵר

tree
etz
עֵץ

shadow
tzel
צֵל

hill
giv'a
גִּבְעָה

road
dereĥ
דֶּרֶךְ

smoke
ashan
עָשָׁן

picnic
piknik
פִּיקְנִיק

ant
nemala
נְמָלָה

dirt
afar
עָפָר

tent
ohel
אוֹהֶל

sky
shama'yim
שָׁמַיִם

train tracks
pasey rakevet
פַּסֵּי רַכֶּבֶת

sleeping bag
sak shena
שַׂק שֵׁנָה

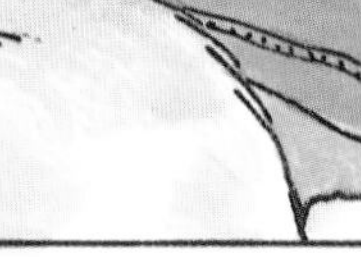

man
gever
גֶּבֶר

woman
isha
אִישָׁה

boy
yeled
יֶלֶד

girl
yalda
יַלְדָּה

baby
tinok
תִּינוֹק

farm
meshek
מֶשֶׁק

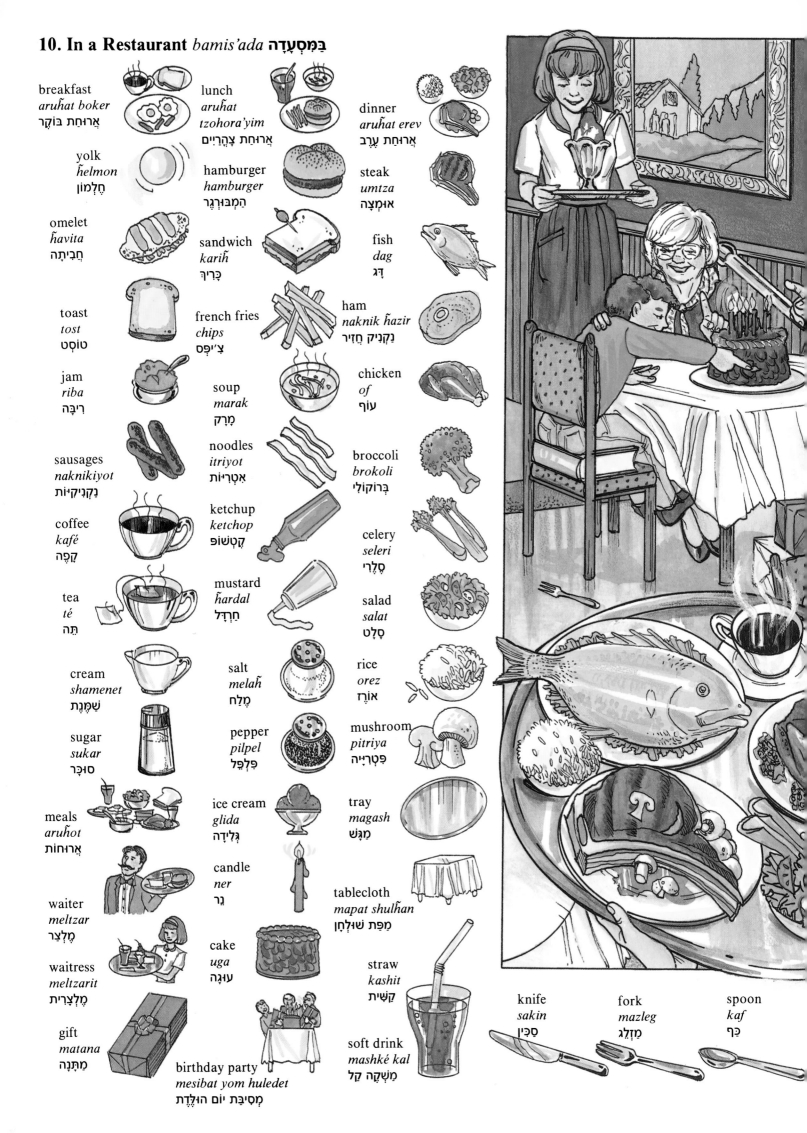

10. In a Restaurant *bamis'ada* בַּמִסְעָדָה

breakfast
aruĥat boker
אֲרוּחַת בּוֹקֶר

yolk
ĥelmon
חֶלְמוֹן

omelet
ĥavita
חֲבִיתָה

toast
tost
טוֹסְט

jam
riba
רִיבָּה

sausages
naknikiyot
נַקְנִיקִיּוֹת

coffee
kafé
קָפֶה

tea
té
תֵּה

cream
shamenet
שַׁמֶּנֶת

sugar
sukar
סוּכָּר

meals
aruĥot
אֲרוּחוֹת

waiter
meltzar
מֶלְצַר

waitress
meltzarit
מֶלְצָרִית

gift
matana
מַתָּנָה

lunch
aruĥat
tzohora'yim
אֲרוּחַת צָהֳרַיִים

hamburger
hamburger
הַמְבּוּרְגֶר

sandwich
kariĥ
כָּרִיךְ

french fries
chips
צִ'יפְּס

soup
marak
מָרָק

noodles
itriyot
אִטְרִיּוֹת

ketchup
ketchop
קֶטְשׁוֹפּ

mustard
ĥardal
חַרְדָּל

salt
melaĥ
מֶלַח

pepper
pilpel
פִּלְפֵּל

ice cream
glida
גְּלִידָה

candle
ner
נֵר

cake
uga
עוּגָה

birthday party
mesibat yom huledet
מְסִיבַּת יוֹם הוּלֶדֶת

dinner
aruĥat erev
אֲרוּחַת עֶרֶב

steak
umtza
אוּמְצָה

fish
dag
דָּג

ham
naknik ĥazir
נַקְנִיק חֲזִיר

chicken
of
עוֹף

broccoli
brokoli
בְּרוֹקוֹלִי

celery
seleri
סֶלֶרִי

salad
salat
סָלָט

rice
orez
אוֹרֶז

mushroom
pitriya
פִּטְרִיָּה

tray
magash
מַגָּשׁ

tablecloth
mapat shulĥan
מַפַּת שׁוּלְחָן

straw
kashit
קַשִּׁית

soft drink
mashké kal
מַשְׁקֶה קַל

knife
sakin
סַכִּין

fork
mazleg
מַזְלֵג

spoon
kaf
כַּף

plate
tzalaħat
צַלַּחַת

saucer
taħtit
תַּחְתִּית

cup
sefel
סֵפֶל

glass
kos
כּוֹס

bowl
ke'ara
קְעָרָה

napkin
mapit
מַפִּית

menu
tafrit
תַּפְרִיט

11. The Doctor's Office *etzel harofé* אֵצֶל הָרוֹפֵא

doctor
rof'a
רוֹפְאָה

nurse
aĥ
אָח

patient
metupal
מְטוּפָּל

medicine
trufa
תְּרוּפָה

pill
kadur
כַּדּוּר

thermometer
madĥom
מַדְחוֹם

bandage
plaster
פְּלַסְטֶר

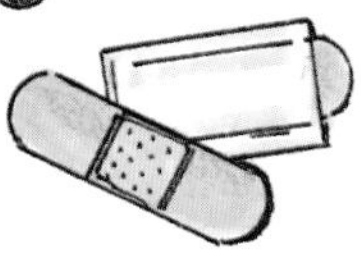

cast
geves
גֶּבֶס

sling
matlé
מַתְלֶה

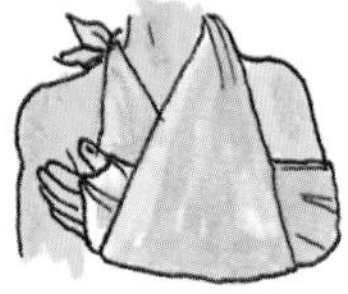

hypodermic needle
mazrek
מַזְרֵק

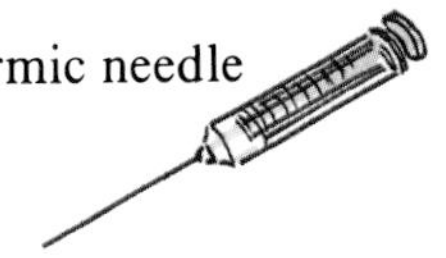

blood
dam
דָּם

cane
makel
מַקֵּל

crutch
kav
קַב

stethoscope
masket
מַסְכֵּת

examining table
shulĥan bdika
שׁוּלְחַן בְּדִיקָה

sneeze
itush
עִיטּוּשׁ

arm
zro'a
זְרוֹעַ

elbow
marpek
מַרְפֵּק

hand
yad
יָד

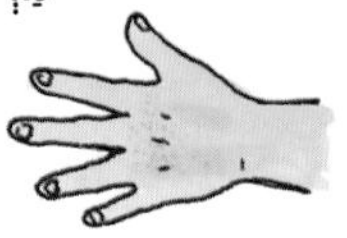

finger
etzba
אֶצְבַּע

thumb
agudal
אֲגוּדָל

leg
regel
רֶגֶל

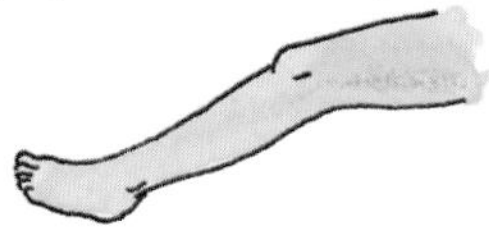

wheelchair
kisé galgalim
כִּיסֵּא גַּלְגַּלִּים

foot
kaf regel
כַּף רֶגֶל

ankle
karsol
קַרְסוֹל

toe
etzba
אֶצְבַּע

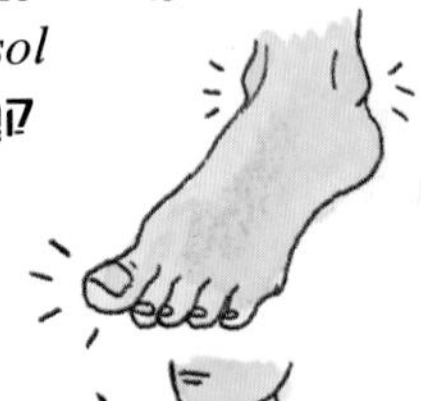

shoulder
katef
כָּתֵף

back
gav
גַּב

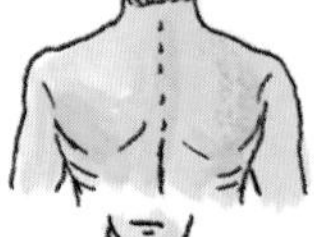

chest
ĥazé
חָזֶה

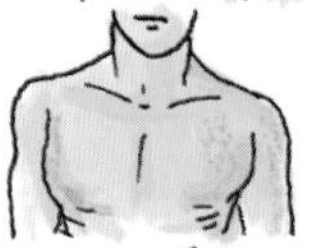

knee
bereĥ
בֶּרֶךְ

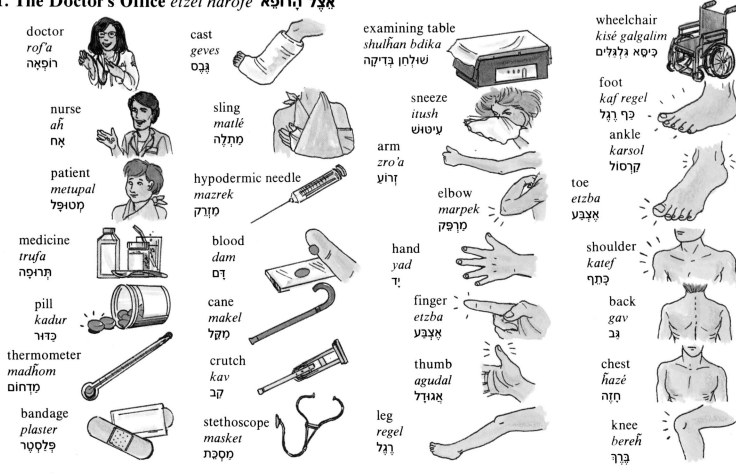

The Dentist's Office *etzel rofé hashina'yim* אֵצֶל רוֹפֵא הַשִּׁינַּיִים

dentist
rofé shina'yim
רוֹפֵא שִׁינַּיִים

dental hygienist
shinanit
שִׁינָּנִית

tooth
shen
שֵׁן

oothbrush
nivreshet shina'yim
מִבְרֶשֶׁת שִׁינַּיִים

toothpaste
mishĥat shina'yim
מִשְׁחַת שִׁינַּיִים

dental floss
ĥut dentali
חוּט דֶּנְטָלִי

waiting room
ĥadar hamtana
חֲדַר הַמְתָּנָה

magazines
kitvey et
כִּתְבֵי עֵת

x ray
tatzlum rentgen
תַּצְלוּם רֶנְטְגֶן

smile
ĥi'yuĥ
חִיּוּךְ

lips
sfata'yim
שְׂפָתַיִים

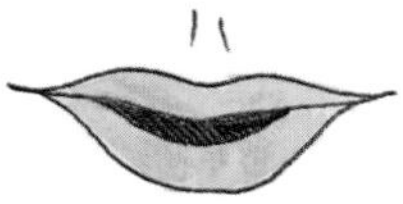

tongue
lashon
לָשׁוֹן

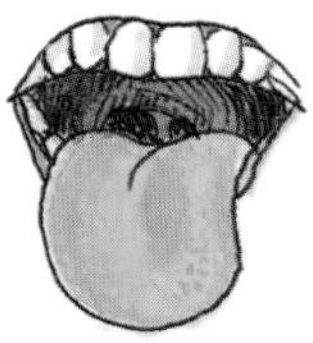

eyebrow
gaba
גַּבָּה

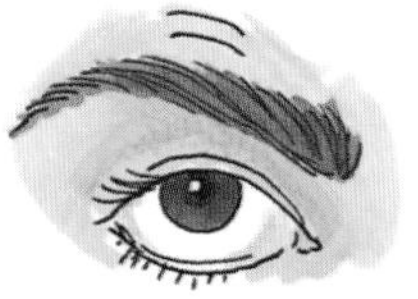

eyes
eyna'yim
עֵינַיִים

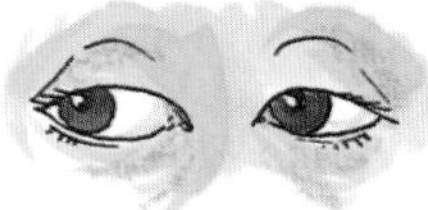

nose
af
אַף

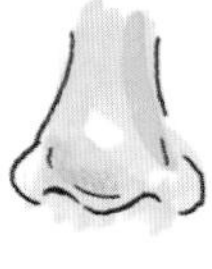

mouth
pé
פֶּה

chin
santer
סַנְטֵר

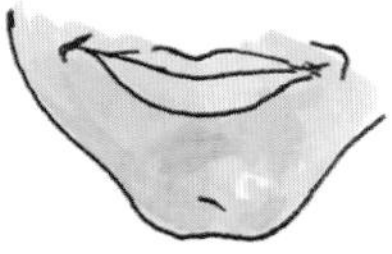

ear
ozen
אוֹזֶן

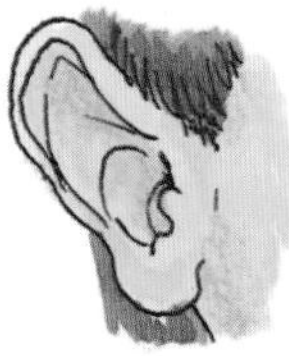

braces
gesher
גֶּשֶׁר

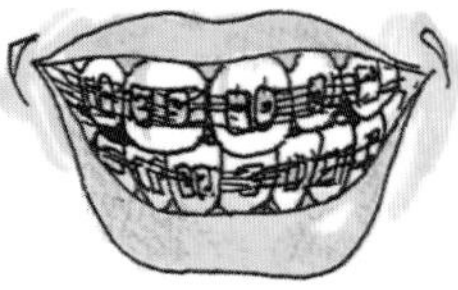

head
rosh
רֹאשׁ

face
panim
פָּנִים

cheek
leĥi
לְחִי

forehead
metzaĥ
מֵצַח

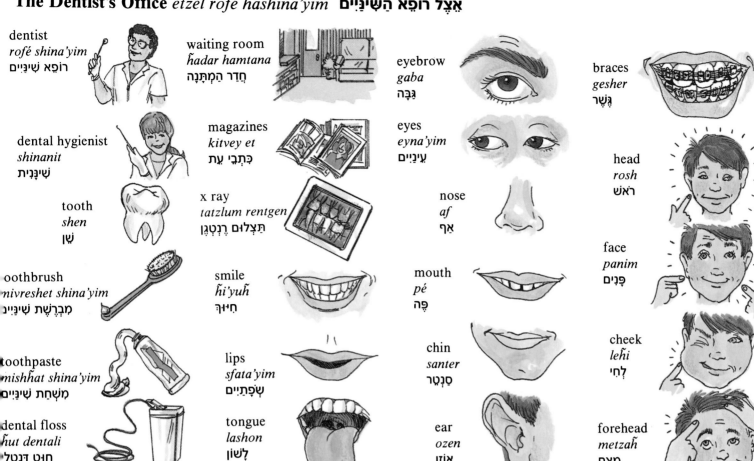

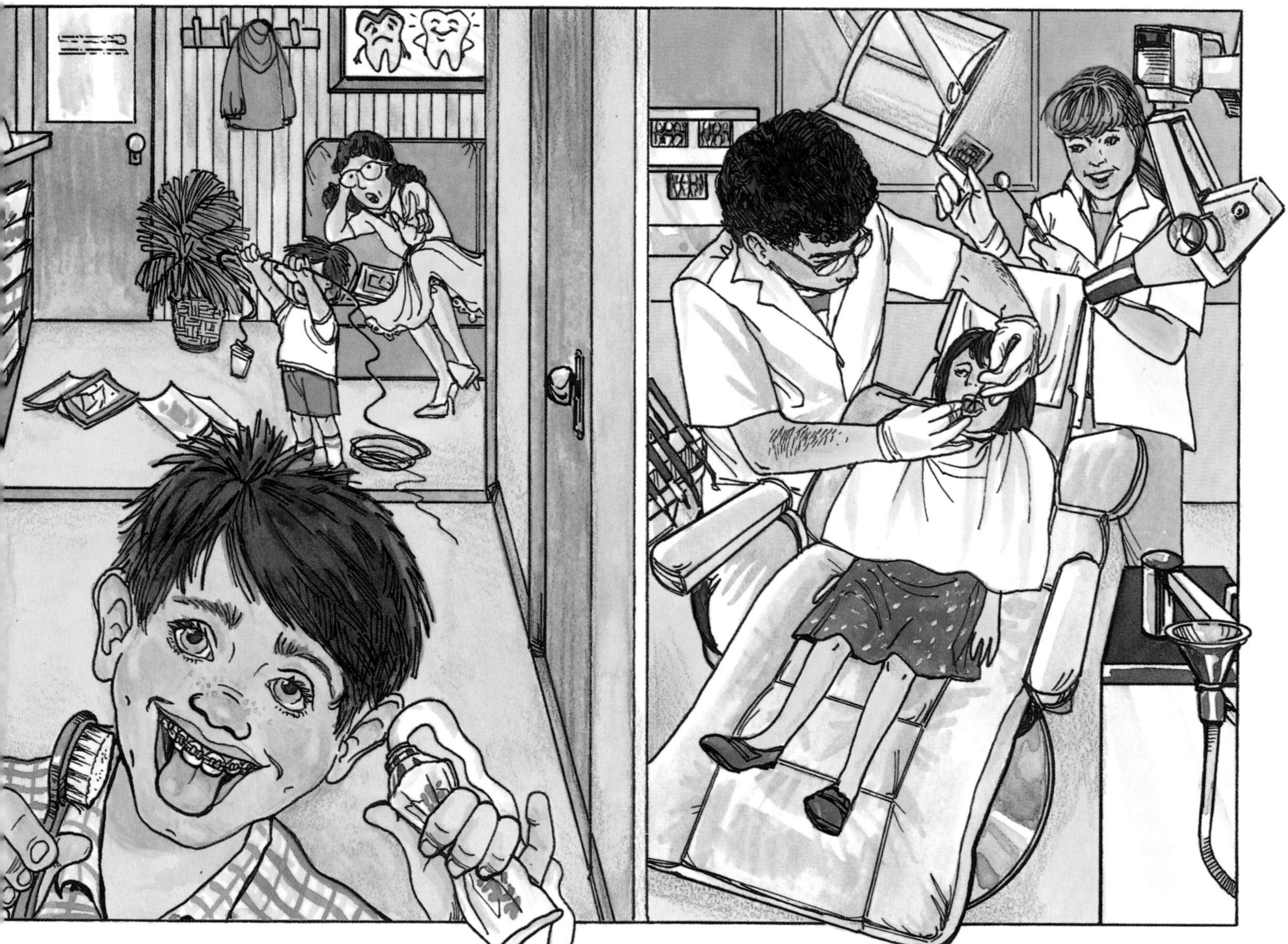

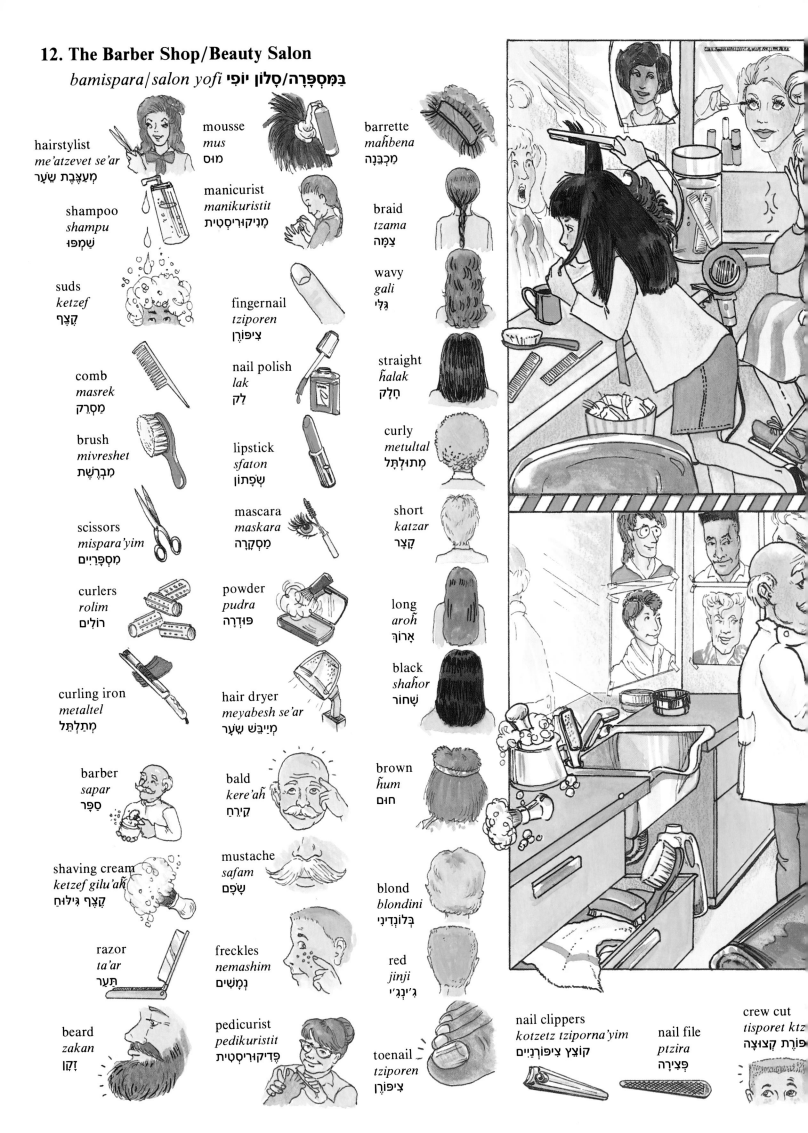

12. The Barber Shop/Beauty Salon

bamispara/salon yofi **בַּמִסְפָּרָה/סָלוֹן יוֹפִי**

hairstylist
me'atzevet se'ar
מְעַצֶּבֶת שֵׂעָר

shampoo
shampu
שַׁמְפּוּ

suds
ketzef
קֶצֶף

comb
masrek
מַסְרֵק

brush
mivreshet
מִבְרֶשֶׁת

scissors
mispara'yim
מִסְפָּרַיִים

curlers
rolim
רוֹלִים

curling iron
metaltel
מְתַלְתֵּל

barber
sapar
סַפָּר

shaving cream
ketzef gilu'aħ
קֶצֶף גִּילּוּחַ

razor
ta'ar
תַּעַר

beard
zakan
זָקָן

mousse
mus
מוּס

manicurist
manikuristit
מָנִיקוּרִיסְטִית

fingernail
tziporen
צִיפּוֹרֶן

nail polish
lak
לַק

lipstick
sfaton
שְׂפָתוֹן

mascara
maskara
מַסְקָרָה

powder
pudra
פּוּדְרָה

hair dryer
meyabesh se'ar
מְיַיבֵּשׁ שֵׂעָר

bald
kere'aħ
קֵירֵחַ

mustache
safam
שָׂפָם

freckles
nemashim
נְמָשִׁים

pedicurist
pedikuristit
פֶּדִיקוּרִיסְטִית

barrette
maħbena
מַכְבֵּנָה

braid
tzama
צַמָּה

wavy
gali
גַּלִּי

straight
ħalak
חָלָק

curly
metultal
מְתוּלְתָּל

short
katzar
קָצָר

long
aroħ
אָרוֹךְ

black
shaħor
שָׁחוֹר

brown
ħum
חוּם

blond
blondini
בְּלוֹנְדִינִי

red
jinji
ג'ינְג'י

toenail
tziporen
צִיפּוֹרֶן

nail clippers
kotzetz tziporna'yim
קוֹצֵץ צִיפּוֹרְנַיִים

nail file
ptzira
פְּצִירָה

crew cut
tisporet ktz
פּוֹרֶת קְצוּצָה

ponytail
kuku
קוקו

bangs
poni
פּוֹנִי

bun
pka'at
פְּקַעַת

part
shvil
שְׁבִיל

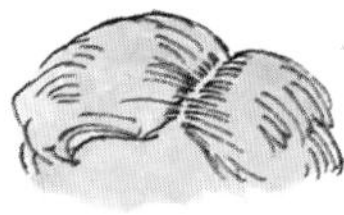

hair spray
tarsis se'ar
תַּרְסִיס שֵׂעָר

hair
se'ar
שֵׂעָר

blow dryer
meyabesh se'ar
מְיַיבֵּשׁ שֵׂעָר

13. The Post Office *bado'ar* בַּדּוֹאַר

packing tape
niyar devek
נְיַיר דֶּבֶק

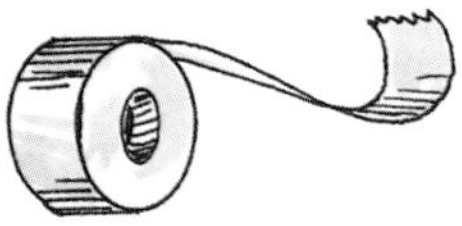

package
ħavila
חֲבִילָה

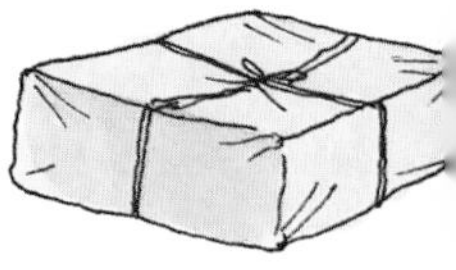

scale
mozna'yim
מֹאזְנַיִים

ink pad
karit dyo
כָּרִית דְּיוֹ

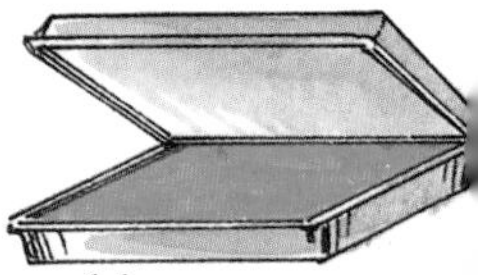

post-office box
ta do'ar
תָּא דּוֹאַר

rubber stamp
ħotemet gumi
חוֹתֶמֶת גּוּמִי

label
pitkit
פִּתְקִית

rubber band
gumiya
גּוּמִיָּה

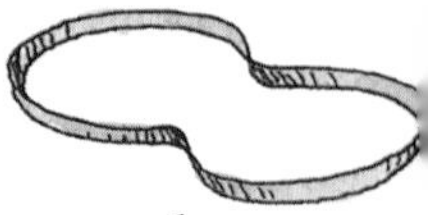

letter
miħtav
מִכְתָּב

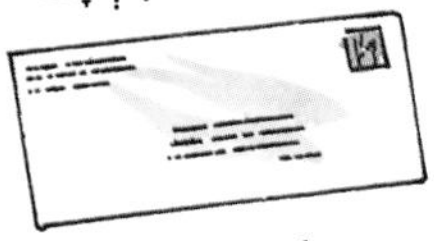

postcard
gluya
גְּלוּיָה

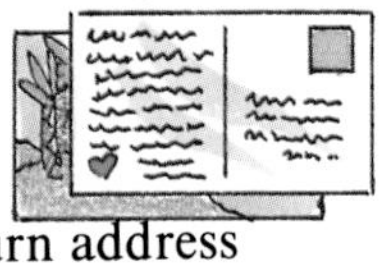

string
ħut
חוּט

knot
kesher
קֶשֶׁר

bow
lula'a
לוּלָאָה

postmark
ħotemet do'ar
חוֹתֶמֶת דּוֹאַר

phone booth
ta telefon
תָּא טֶלֶפוֹן

return address
ktovet hashole'aħ
כְּתוֹבֶת הַשּׁוֹלֵחַ

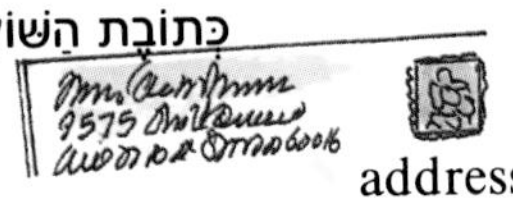

address
ktovet
כְּתוֹבֶת

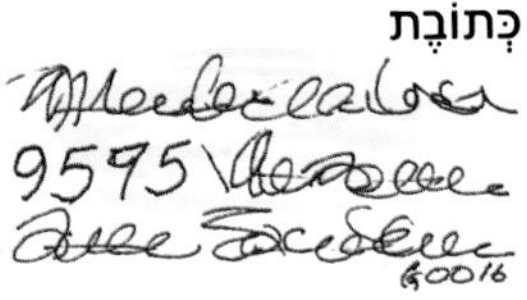

mailbox
teyvat do'ar
תֵּיבַת דּוֹאַר

zip code
mikud
מִיקוּד

mail slot
ħaritz
חָרִיץ

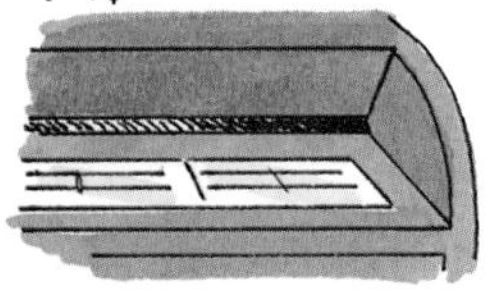

mailbag
sak do'ar
שַׂק דּוֹאַר

postal worker
davar
דַּוָּור

stamp
bul
בּוּל

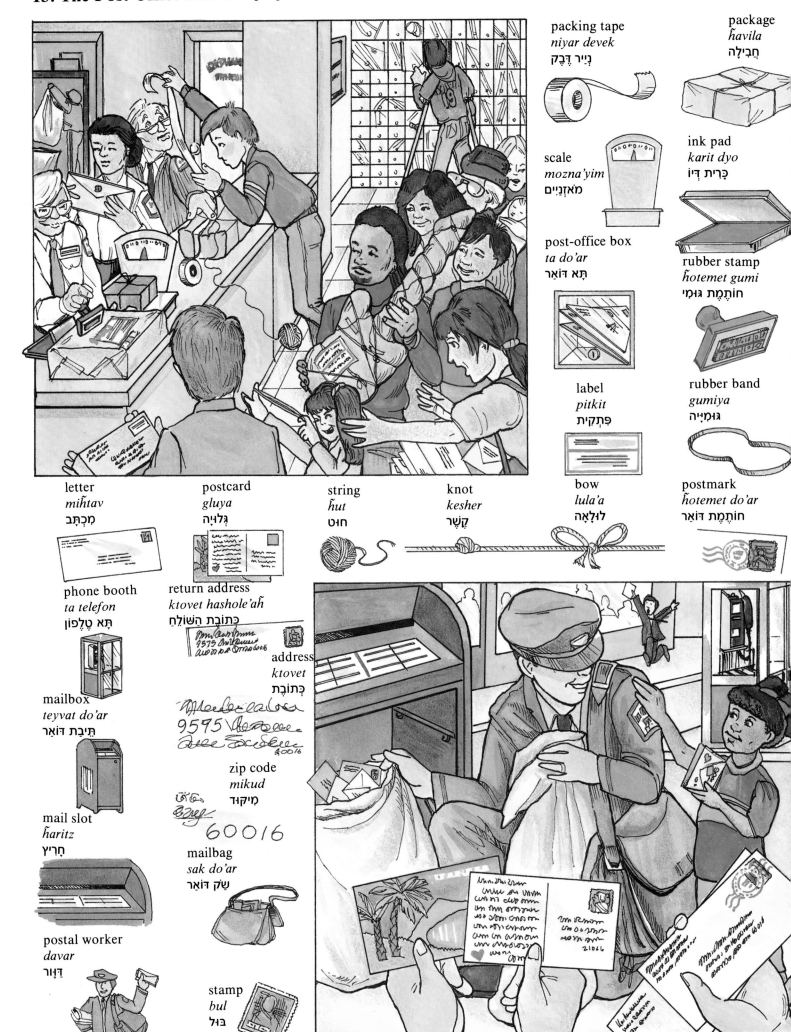

The Bank *babank* בַּבַּנְק

paper clip
mehadek
מְהַדֵּק

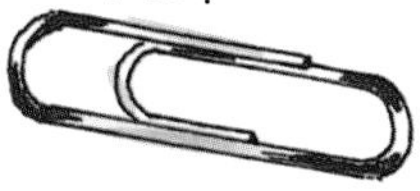

security guard
ish bitaȟon
אִישׁ בִּיטָּחוֹן

security camera
matzlemat bitaȟon
מַצְלֵמַת בִּיטָּחוֹן

safe
ȟadar kasafot
חֲדַר כַּסָּפוֹת

credit card
kartis ashray
כַּרְטִיס אַשְׁרַאי

typewriter
meȟonat ktiva
מְכוֹנַת כְּתִיבָה

safety deposit box
kaséfet
כַּסֶּפֶת

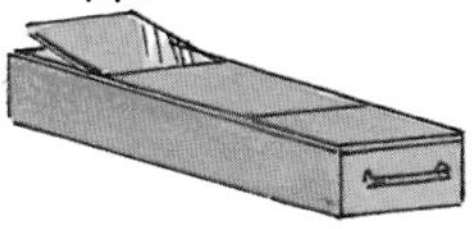

notepad
dafdefet
דַּפְדֶּפֶת

teller
pkid bank
פְּקִיד בַּנְק

wallet
arnak
אַרְנָק

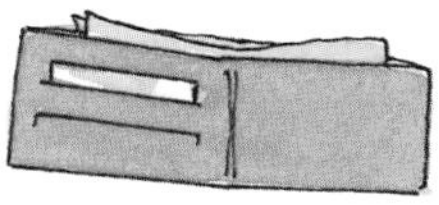

key
mafté'aȟ
מַפְתֵּחַ

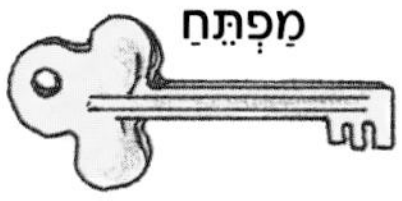

lock
man'ul
מַנְעוּל

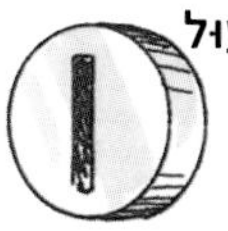

file cabinet
aron tiyuk
אֲרוֹן תִּיּוּק

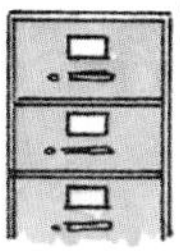

receptionist
pkidat kabala
פְּקִידַת קַבָּלָה

bill
shtar
שְׁטָר

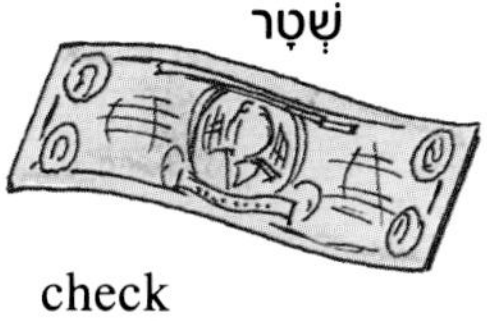

coin
matbe'a
מַטְבֵּעַ

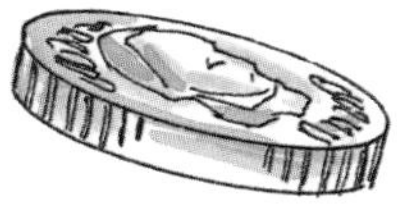

check
hamȟa'a
הַמְחָאָה

checkbook
pinkas hamȟa'ot
פִּנְקַס הַמְחָאוֹת

piggy bank
kupat ȟisaȟon
קוּפַּת חִיסָּכוֹן

signature
ȟatima
חֲתִימָה

drive-in
bank drayv-in
בַּנְק דְּרַיְב-אִין

automatic teller
kaspomat
כַּסְפּוֹמָט

14. At the Gas Station *betaȟanat hadelek* בְּתַחֲנַת הַדֶּלֶק

mechanic
meȟonay
מְכוֹנַאי

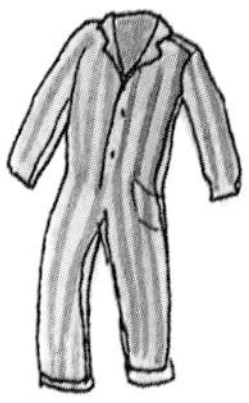
coveralls
sarbal
סַרְבָּל

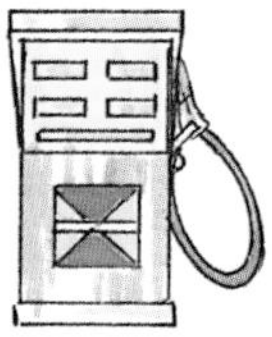
gas pump
mash'evat delek
מַשְׁאֵבַת דֶּלֶק

race car
meȟonit merotz
מְכוֹנִית מֵירוֹץ

pliers
pla'yer
פְּלַיֶר

oil
shemen
שֶׁמֶן

rag
smartut
סְמַרְטוּט

sunroof
gag niftaȟ
גַּג נִפְתָּח

dashboard
lu'aȟ she'onim
לוּחַ שְׁעוֹנִים

garage
musaȟ
מוּסָךְ

tow truck
masa'it grar
מַשָּׂאִית גְּרָר

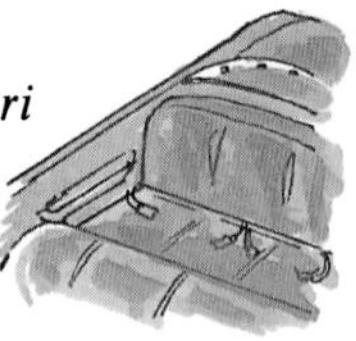
backseat
moshav aȟori
מוֹשָׁב אֲחוֹרִי

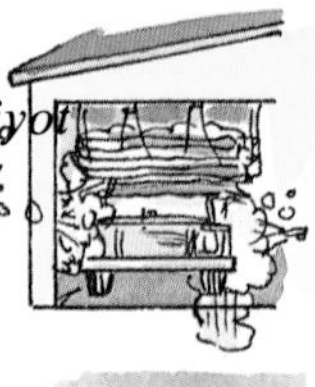
car wash
shtifat meȟoniyot
שְׁטִיפַת מְכוֹנִיּוֹת

truck driver
nahag masa'it
נַהַג מַשָּׂאִית

driver's seat
moshav hanéhag
מוֹשַׁב הַנֶּהָג

gas cap
miȟsé delek
מִכְסֵה דֶּלֶק

passenger's seat
moshav kidmi
מוֹשָׁב קִדְמִי

tank truck
meȟalit
מְכָלִית

tricycle
tlat ofan
תְּלַת אוֹפַן

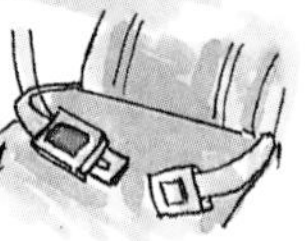
seat belt
ȟagorat betiȟut
חֲגוֹרַת בְּטִיחוּת

bicycle
ofana'yim
אוֹפַנַּיִם

handlebars
kidon
כִּידוֹן

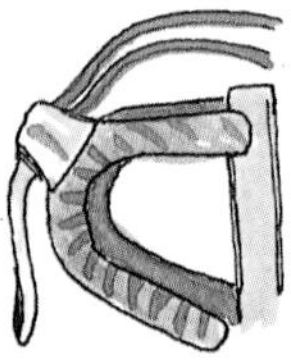
hand brake
ma'atzor yad
מַעְצוֹר יָד

hood
miȟsé hamano'a
מִכְסֵה הַמָּנוֹעַ

engine
mano'a
מָנוֹעַ

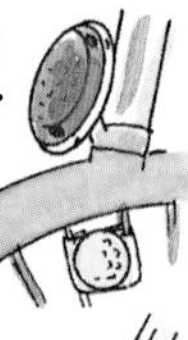
reflectors
maȟzir or
מַחֲזִיר אוֹר

bicycle chain
sharsheret
שַׁרְשֶׁרֶת

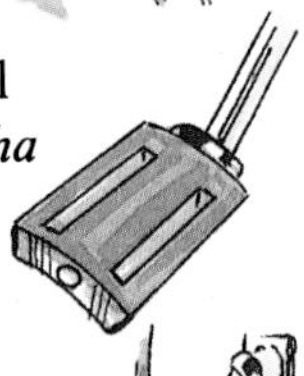
pedal
davsha
דַּוְשָׁה

trunk
ta mit'an
תָּא מִטְעָן

spokes
ȟishurim
חִישׁוּרִים

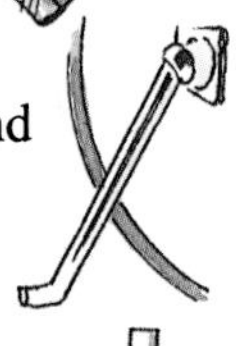
kickstand
raglit
רַגְלִית

fender
pagosh
פָּגוֹשׁ

training wheels
galgaley ezer
גַּלְגַּלֵּי עֵזֶר

jack
magbeha
מַגְבֵּהָה

flat tire
teker
תֶּקֶר

tire
tzmig
צְמִיג

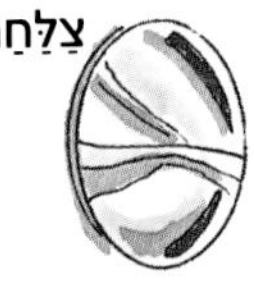
hubcap
tzalaȟat
צַלַּחַת

headligh
or kidmi
אוֹר קִדְמִי

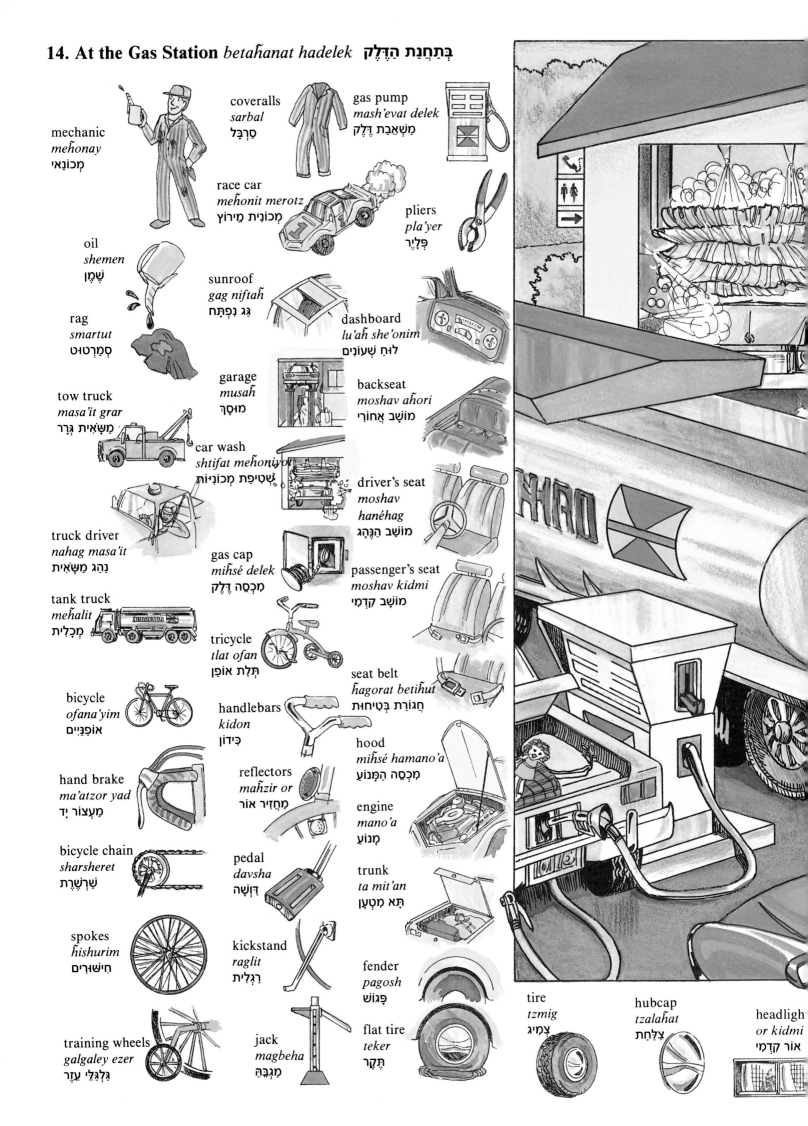

brake lights
orot atzira
אוֹרוֹת עֲצִירָה

windshield
ĥalon kidmi
חַלּוֹן קִדְמִי

windshield wipers
magévim
מַגְּבִים

steering wheel
hegé
הֶגֶה

rearview mirror
mar'a aĥorit
מַרְאָה אֲחוֹרִית

air hose
tzinor avir
צִינּוֹר אֲוִויר

door handle
yadit
יָדִית

15. People in Our Community *anashim bakehila* אֲנָשִׁים בַּקְּהִילָּה

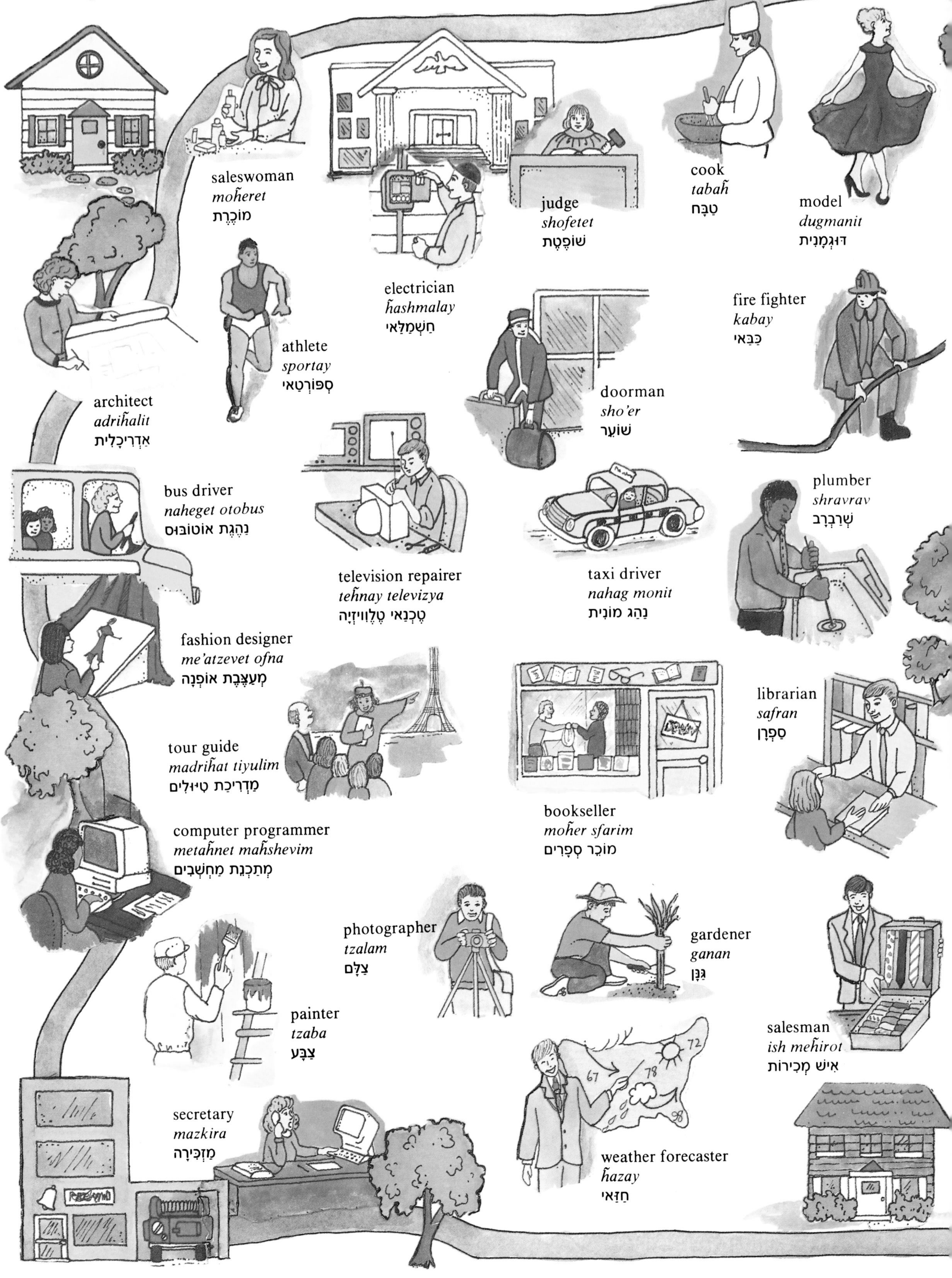

saleswoman
*mo**h**eret*
מוֹכֶרֶת
judge
shofetet
שׁוֹפֶטֶת
cook
*taba**h***
טַבָּח
model
dugmanit
דוּגְמָנִית
electrician
***h**ashmalay*
חַשְׁמַלַּאי
athlete
sportay
סְפּוֹרְטַאי
architect
*adri**h**alit*
אַדְרִיכָלִית
fire fighter
kabay
כַּבַּאי
doorman
sho'er
שׁוֹעֵר
bus driver
naheget otobus
נַהֶגֶת אוֹטוֹבּוּס
plumber
shravrav
שְׁרַבְרָב
taxi driver
nahag monit
נֶהַג מוֹנִית
television repairer
*te**h**nay televizya*
טֶכְנַאי טֶלֶוִיזְיָה
fashion designer
me'atzevet ofna
מְעַצֶּבֶת אוֹפְנָה
librarian
safran
סַפְרָן
tour guide
*madri**h**at tiyulim*
מַדְרִיכַת טִיּוּלִים
bookseller
*mo**h**er sfarim*
מוֹכֵר סְפָרִים
computer programmer
*meta**h**net ma**h**shevim*
מְתַכְנֶתֶת מַחְשְׁבִים
photographer
tzalam
צַלָּם
gardener
ganan
גַּנָּן
painter
tzaba
צַבָּע
salesman
*ish me**h**irot*
אִישׁ מְכִירוֹת
secretary
mazkira
מַזְכִּירָה
weather forecaster
***h**azay*
חַזַּאי

policewoman
shoteret
שׁוֹטֶרֶת
veterinarian
veterinar
וֶטֶרִינָר
disc jockey
taklitan
תַּקְלִיטָן
reporter
katav
כַּתָּב
construction worker
banay
בַּנַּאי
florist
moȟeret praȟim
מוֹכֶרֶת פְּרָחִים
tailor
ȟayat
חַיָּט
factory worker
po'el
פּוֹעֵל
optician
optika'it
אוֹפְּטִיקָאִית
butcher
katzav
קַצָּב
jeweler
taȟshitan
תַּכְשִׁיטָן
foreman
menahel avoda
מְנַהֵל עֲבוֹדָה
carpenter
nagar
נַגָּר
banker
banka'it
בַּנְקָאִית
artist
oman
אָמָּן
pharmacist
rokaȟat
רוֹקַחַת
sailor
yamay
יַמַּאי
lawyer
oreȟet din
עוֹרֶכֶת דִּין
paramedic
ȟovesh
חוֹבֵשׁ
letter carrier
davar
דַּוָּר
fisherman
dayag
דַּיָּג
cowboy
boker
בּוֹקֵר
policeman
shoter
שׁוֹטֵר
astronomer
astronom
אַסְטְרוֹנוֹם

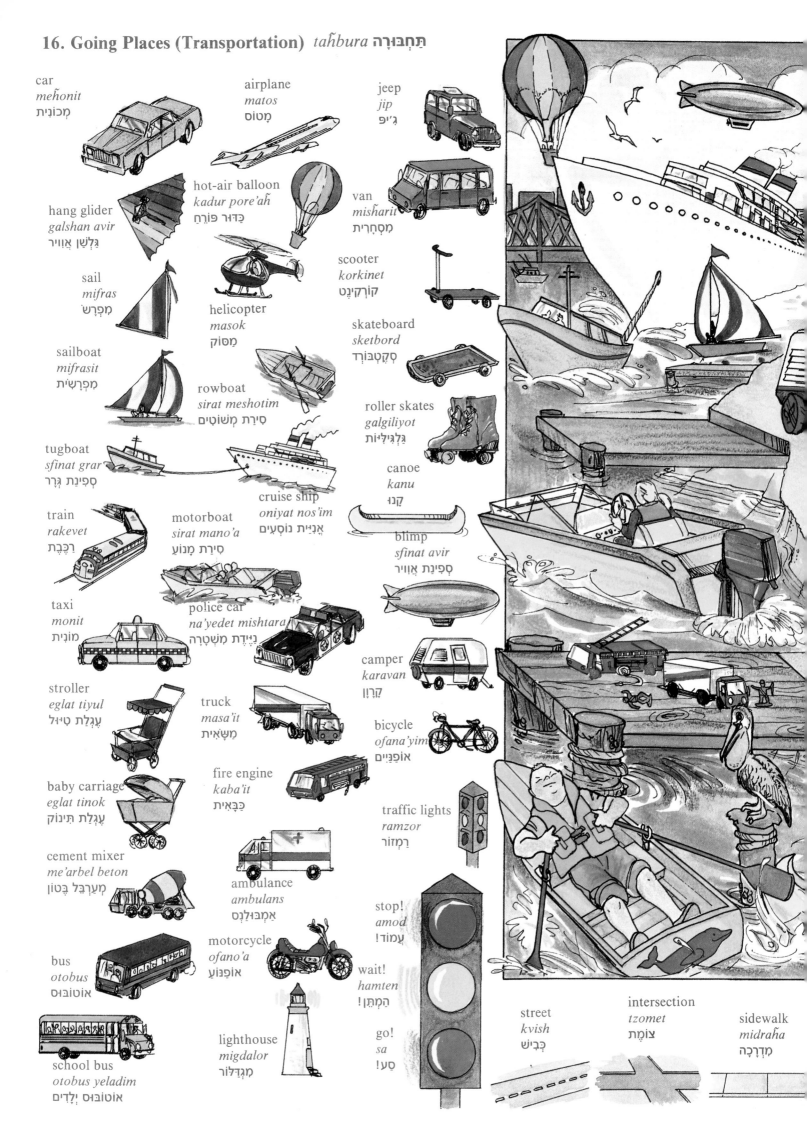

16. Going Places (Transportation) *taĥbura* תַּחְבּוּרָה

car
meĥonit
מְכוֹנִית

hang glider
galshan avir
גַּלְשַׁן אֲוִויר

sail
mifras
מִפְרָשׂ

sailboat
mifrasit
מִפְרָשִׂית

tugboat
sfinat grar
סְפִינַת גְּרָר

train
rakevet
רַכֶּבֶת

taxi
monit
מוֹנִית

stroller
eglat tiyul
עֶגְלַת טִיּוּל

baby carriage
eglat tinok
עֶגְלַת תִּינוֹק

cement mixer
me'arbel beton
מְעַרְבֵּל בֶּטוֹן

bus
otobus
אוֹטוֹבּוּס

school bus
otobus yeladim
אוֹטוֹבּוּס יְלָדִים

airplane
matos
מָטוֹס

hot-air balloon
kadur pore'aĥ
כַּדּוּר פּוֹרֵחַ

helicopter
masok
מַסּוֹק

rowboat
sirat meshotim
סִירַת מְשׁוֹטִים

cruise ship
oniyat nos'im
אֳנִיַּת נוֹסְעִים

motorboat
sirat mano'a
סִירַת מָנוֹעַ

police car
na'yedet mishtara
נַיֶּדֶת מִשְׁטָרָה

truck
masa'it
מַשָּׂאִית

fire engine
kaba'it
כַּבָּאִית

ambulance
ambulans
אַמְבּוּלַנְס

motorcycle
ofano'a
אוֹפַנּוֹעַ

lighthouse
migdalor
מִגְדַּלּוֹר

jeep
jip
גִ'יפּ

van
misĥarit
מִסְחָרִית

scooter
korkinet
קוֹרְקִינֶט

skateboard
sketbord
סְקֶטְבּוֹרְד

roller skates
galgiliyot
גַּלְגִּילִיּוֹת

canoe
kanu
קָנוּ

blimp
sfinat avir
סְפִינַת אֲוִויר

camper
karavan
קָרָוָן

bicycle
ofana'yim
אוֹפַנַּיִם

traffic lights
ramzor
רַמְזוֹר

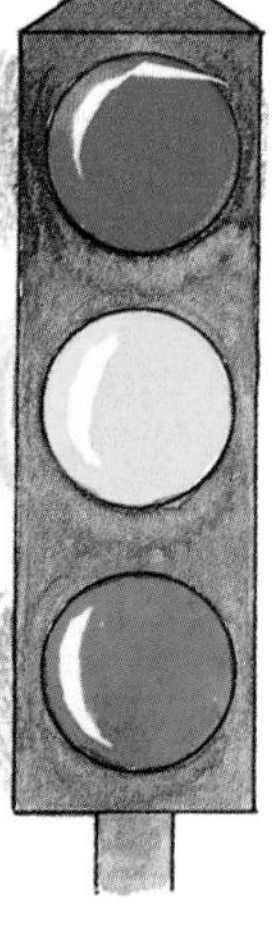

stop!
amod
!עֲמוֹד

wait!
hamten
!הַמְתֵּן

go!
sa
!סַע

street
kvish
כְּבִישׁ

intersection
tzomet
צֹמֶת

sidewalk
midraĥa
מִדְרָכָה

dock
mezaĥ
מֶזַח

bus stop
taĥanat otobus
תַּחֲנַת אוֹטוֹבּוּס

bridge
gesher
גֶּשֶׁר

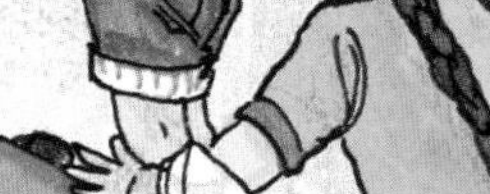

crosswalk
ma'avar ĥatziya
מַעֲבַר חֲצִיָּה

oar
mashot
מָשׁוֹט

boat
sfina
סְפִינָה

stop sign
tamrur atzor
תַּמְרוּר עֲצוֹר

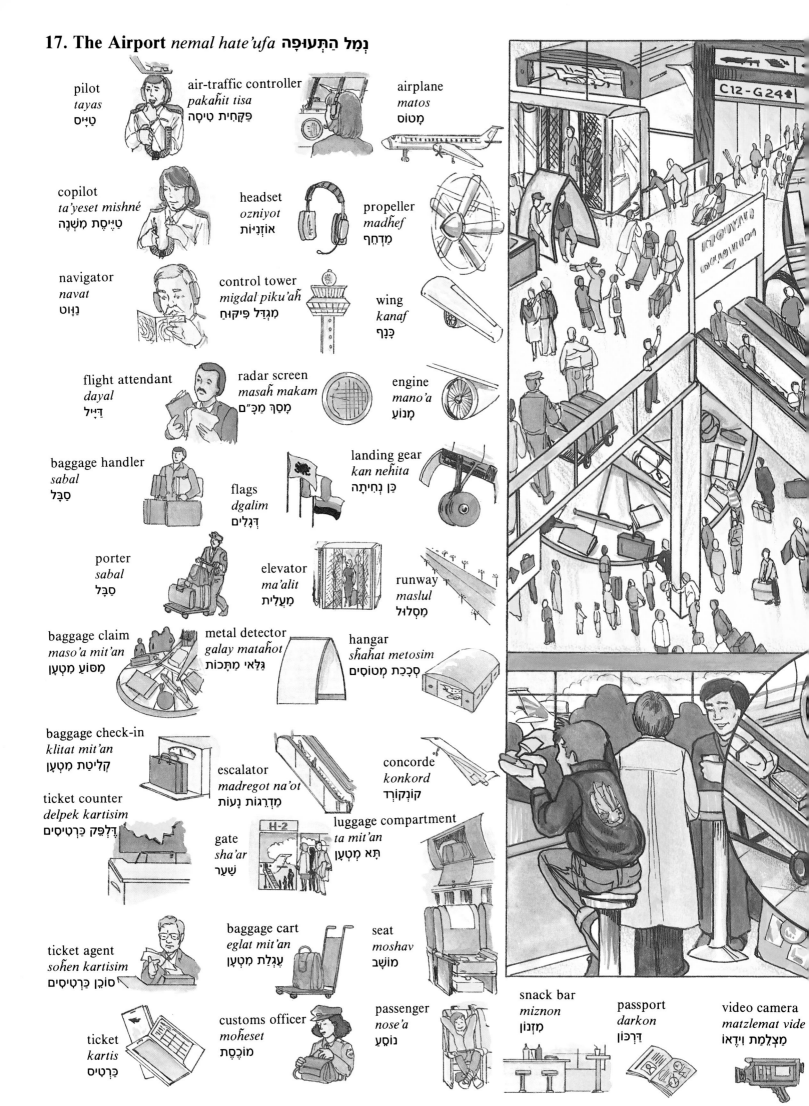

17. The Airport *nemal hate'ufa* נְמַל הַתְּעוּפָה

pilot
tayas
טַיָּס

air-traffic controller
pakaĥit tisa
פַּקָּחִית טִיסָה

airplane
matos
מָטוֹס

copilot
ta'yeset mishné
טַיֶּסֶת מִשְׁנֶה

headset
ozniyot
אוֹזְנִיּוֹת

propeller
madĥef
מַדְחֵף

navigator
navat
נַוָּט

control tower
migdal piku'aĥ
מִגְדַּל פִּיקּוּחַ

wing
kanaf
כָּנָף

flight attendant
dayal
דַּיָּל

radar screen
masaĥ makam
מָסַךְ מַכָּ"ם

engine
mano'a
מָנוֹעַ

baggage handler
sabal
סַבָּל

flags
dgalim
דְּגָלִים

landing gear
kan neĥita
כַּן נְחִיתָה

porter
sabal
סַבָּל

elevator
ma'alit
מַעֲלִית

runway
maslul
מַסְלוּל

baggage claim
maso'a mit'an
מַסּוֹעַ מִטְעָן

metal detector
galay mataĥot
גַּלַּאי מַתָּכוֹת

hangar
sĥaĥat metosim
סְכָכַת מְטוֹסִים

baggage check-in
klitat mit'an
קְלִיטַת מִטְעָן

escalator
madregot na'ot
מַדְרֵגוֹת נָעוֹת

concorde
konkord
קוֹנְקוֹרְד

ticket counter
delpek kartisim
דֶּלְפֵּק כַּרְטִיסִים

gate
sha'ar
שַׁעַר

luggage compartment
ta mit'an
תָּא מִטְעָן

ticket agent
soĥen kartisim
סוֹכֵן כַּרְטִיסִים

baggage cart
eglat mit'an
עֶגְלַת מִטְעָן

seat
moshav
מוֹשָׁב

ticket
kartis
כַּרְטִיס

customs officer
moĥeset
מוֹכֶסֶת

passenger
nose'a
נוֹסֵעַ

snack bar
miznon
מִזְנוֹן

passport
darkon
דַּרְכּוֹן

video camera
matzlemat vide
מַצְלֵמַת וִידֵאוֹ

nnis racket
aĥbet tenis
מַחְבֵּט טֶנִ

binoculars
mishkefet
מִשְׁקֶפֶת

camera
matzlema
מַצְלֵמָה

purse
tik yad
תִּיק יָד

suitcase
mizvada
מִזְוָודָה

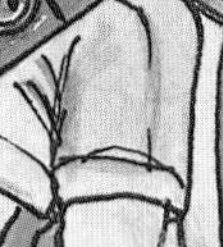

garment bag
minsa bgadim
מִנְשָׂא בְּגָדִים

briefcase
tik menahalim
תִּיק מְנַהֲלִים

18. Sports *sport* סְפּוֹרְט

gymnastics
hit'amlut
הִתְעַמְּלוּת

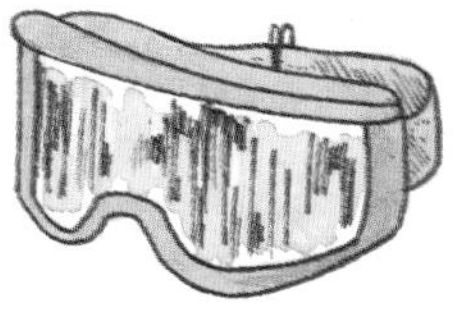

goggles
mishkefey s̃hiya
מִשְׁקְפֵי שְׂחִיָּה

wrestling
he'avkut
הֵיאָבְקוּת

cross-country skiing
cros kantri ski'ing
קְרוֹס קַנְטְרִי סְקִיאִינְג

cycling
rẽhiva al ofana'yim
רְכִיבָה עַל אוֹפַנַּיִים

soccer
kaduregel
כַּדּוּרֶגֶל

long jump
kfitza laroh̃ak
קְפִיצָה לָרוֹחַק

car racing
merotz meh̃oniyot
מֵירוֹץ מְכוֹנִיּוֹת

baseball
kadur beysbol
כַּדּוּר בֵּייסְבּוֹל

boxing
igruf
אִגְרוּף

badminton
kadur notzit
כַּדּוּר נוֹצִית

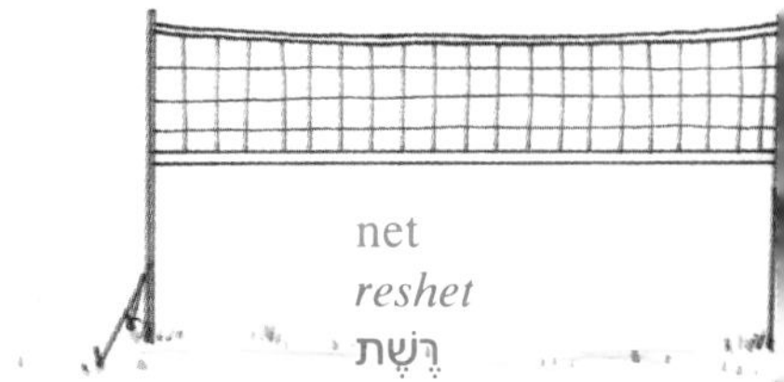

net
reshet
רֶשֶׁת

skates
mah̃lika'yim
מַחֲלִיקַיים

skating
hah̃laka
הַחְלָקָה

hurdles
mesuh̃ot
מְשׂוּכוֹת

football
futbol
פוּטְבּוֹל

golf
golf
גּוֹלְף

medal
medalya
מֶדַלְיָה

horseback riding
rẽhiva al susim
רְכִיבָה עַל סוּסִים

baseball
beysbol
בֵּייסְבּוֹל

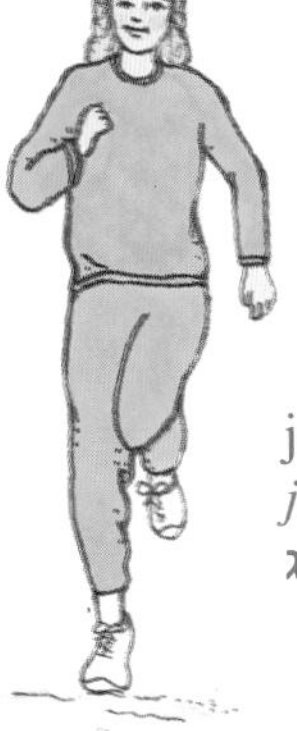

jogging
joging
ג'וֹגִינְג

hockey
hoki
הוֹקִי

tennis
tenis
טֶנִיס

diving
kfitza lama'yim
קְפִיצָה לַמַּיִם

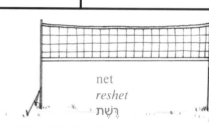

weight lifting
haramat mishkolot
הֲרָמַת מִשְׁקוֹלוֹת

umpire
shofet
שׁוֹפֵט

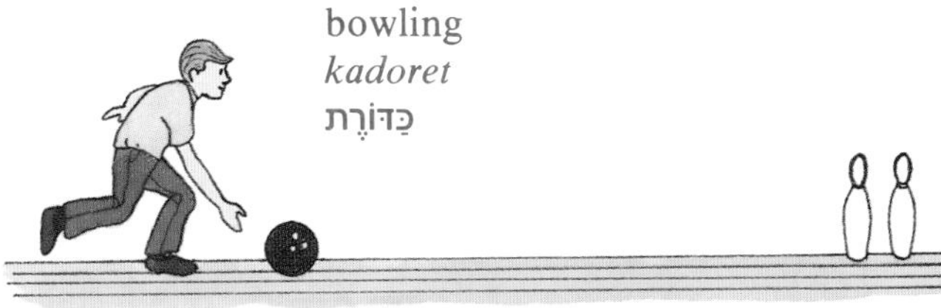

bowling
kadoret
כַּדּוֹרֶת

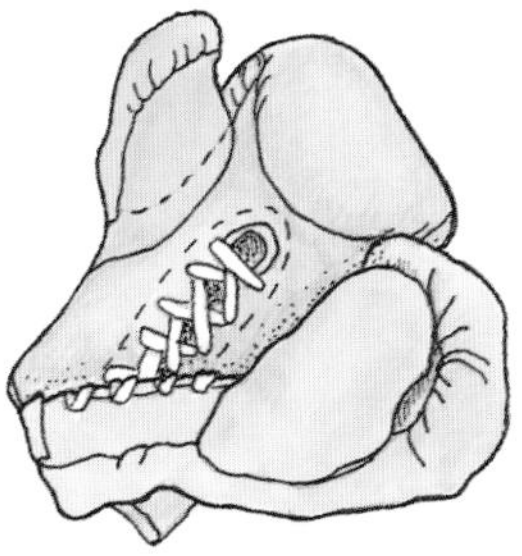

boxing gloves
kfafot igruf
כְּפָפוֹת אֶגְרוֹף

high jump
kfitza lagova
קְפִיצָה לַגּוֹבַהּ

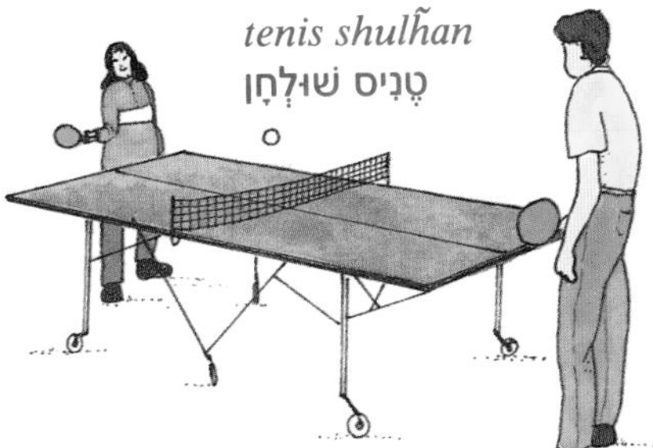

table tennis
tenis shulĥan
טֶנִיס שׁוּלְחָן

skydiving
tzniĥa ĥofshit
צְנִיחָה חוֹפְשִׁית

soccer ball
kaduregel
כַּדּוּרֶגֶל

bat
ala
אַלָּה

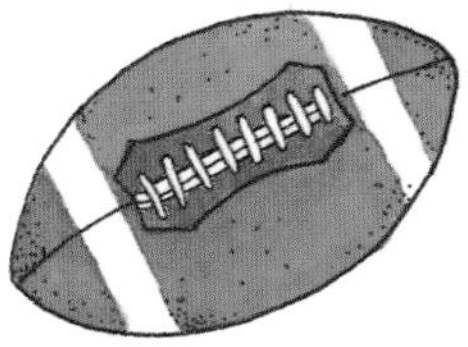

football
kadur futbol
כַּדּוּר פוּטְבּוֹל

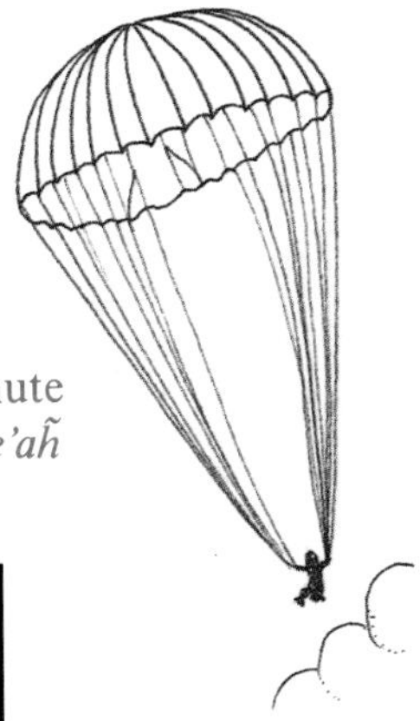

parachute
matzne'aĥ
מַצְנֵחַ

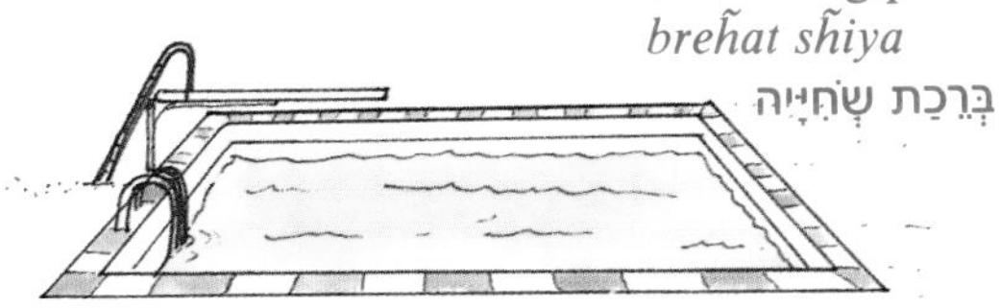

swimming pool
breĥat sĥiya
בְּרֵכַת שְׂחִיָּיה

downhill skiing
glisha
גְּלִישָׁה

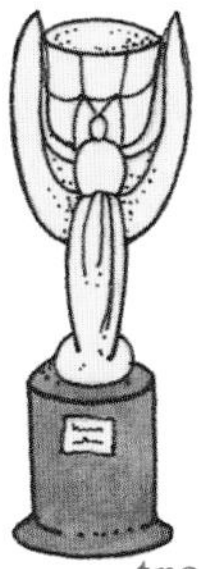

golf club
alat golf
אַלַּת גּוֹלְף

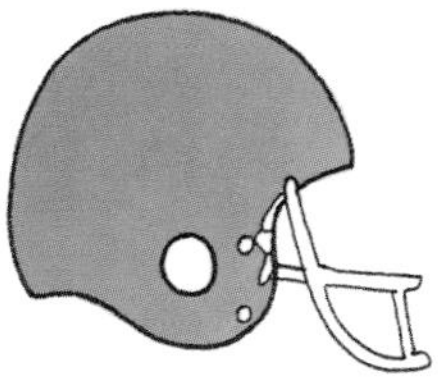

trophy
gavi'a
גָּבִיעַ

running
ritza
רִיצָה

helmet
kasda
קַסְדָּה

horse racing
merotz susim
מֵירוֹץ סוּסִים

bicycle
ofana'yim
אוֹפַנַּיִים

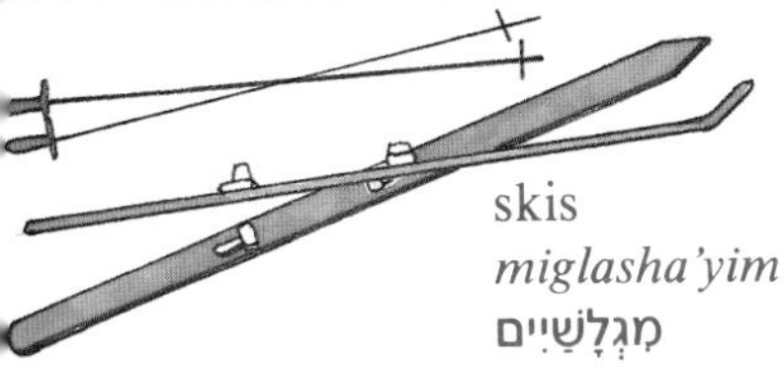

skis
miglasha'yim
מִגְלָשַׁיִים

sailing
haflaga
הַפְלָגָה

basketball
kadursal
כַּדּוּרְסַל

volleyball
kadur'af
כַּדּוּרְעָף

racket
maĥbet
מַחְבֵּט

swimming
sĥiya
שְׂחִיָּיה

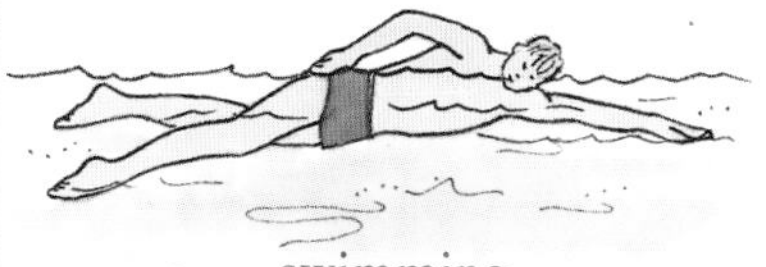

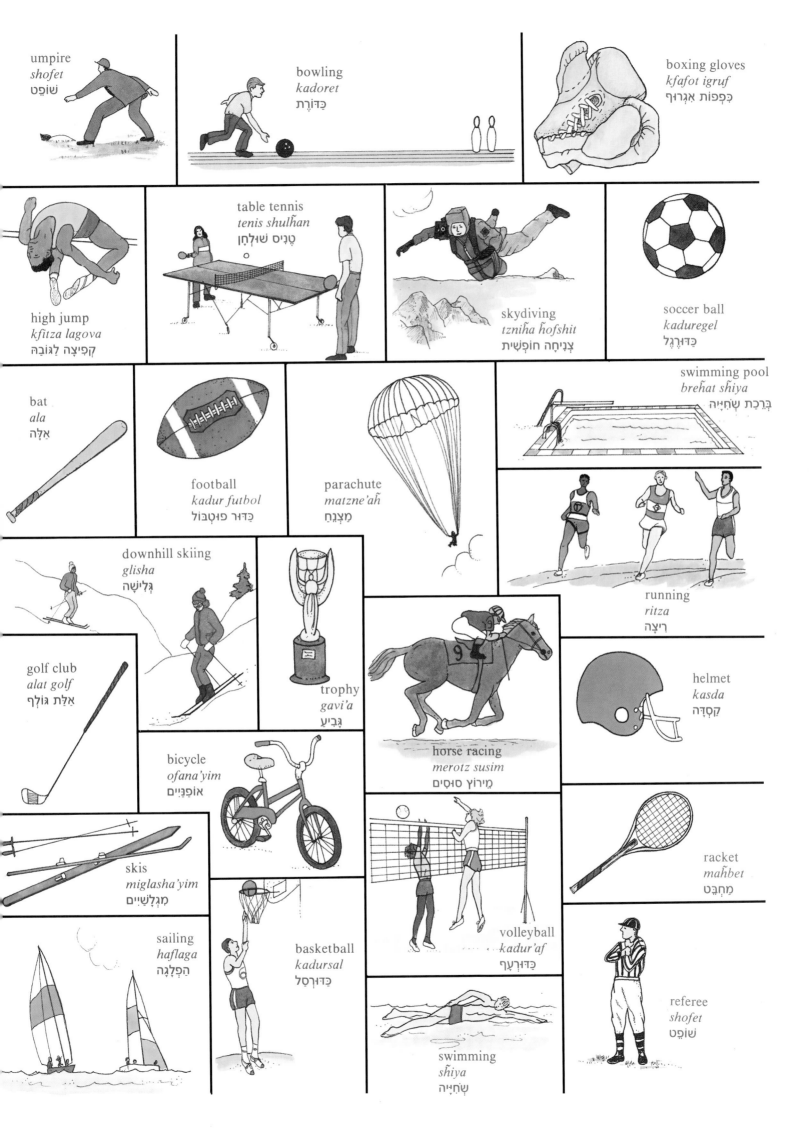

referee
shofet
שׁוֹפֵט

19. The Talent Show *mofa hakishronot* מוֹפָע הַכִּשְׁרוֹנוֹת

actor
saĥkan
שַׂחְקָן

actress
saĥkanit
שַׂחְקָנִית

children
yeladim
יְלָדִים

auditorium
ulam
אוּלָם

audience
kahal
קָהָל

singer
zamar
זַמָּר

stage
bama
בָּמָה
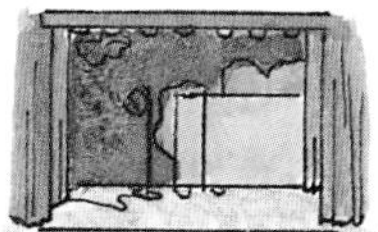

curtain
masaĥ
מָסָךְ
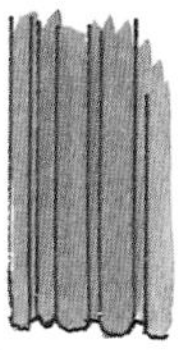

dancer
rakdanit
רַקְדָנִית

scenery
taf'ura
תַּפְאוּרָה

script
tasrit
תַּסְרִיט

ballet slippers
na'aley balet
נַעֲלֵי בַּלֶּט
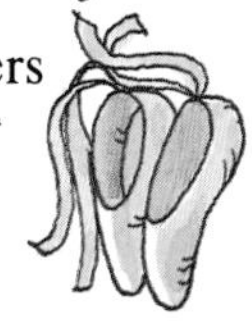

spotlight
zrakor
זַרְקוֹר
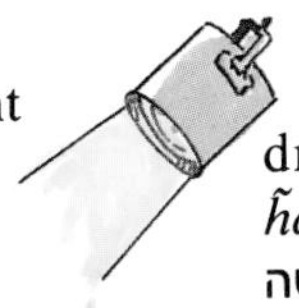

dressing room
ĥadar halbasha
חֲדַר הַלְבָּשָׁה

tutu
ĥatza'it balet
חֲצָאִית בַּלֶּט

rope
ĥevel
חֶבֶל

sewing machine
meĥonat tfira
מְכוֹנַת תְּפִירָה
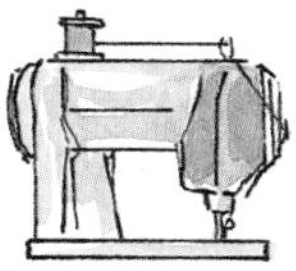

leotard
beged guf
בֶּגֶד גּוּף

microphone
mikrofon
מִיקְרוֹפוֹן

master of ceremonies
manĥé
מַנְחֶה

costume
tilboshet
תִּלְבּוֹשֶׁת

makeup
ipur
אִיפּוּר

orchestra pit
moshav hatizmoret
מוֹשַׁב הַתִּזְמוֹרֶת

mask
maseĥa
מַסֵּכָה

sheet music
dapey tavim
דַּפֵּי תָּוִים

orchestra
tizmoret
תִּזְמוֹרֶת

wig
pe'a
פֵּאָה

conductor
menatze'aĥ
מְנַצֵּחַ

accordion
akordyon
אַקּוֹרְדְיוֹן

cymbals
metzilta'yim
מְצִלְתַּיִים
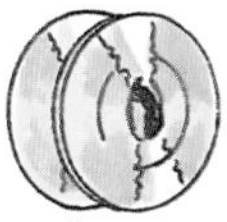

trumpet
ĥatzotzra
חֲצוֹצְרָה

saxophone
saksofon
סַקְסוֹפוֹן

French horn
keren ya'ar
קֶרֶן יַעַר

piano
psanter
פְּסַנְתֵּר

xylophone
ksilofon
קְסִילוֹפוֹן

violin
kinor
כִּינּוֹר
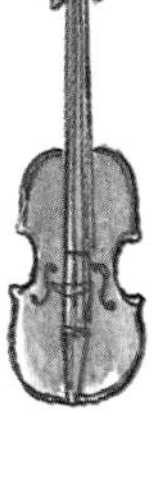

bow
keshet
קֶשֶׁת

guitar
gitara
גִּיטָרָה
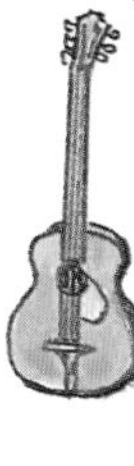

drum
tof
תּוֹף

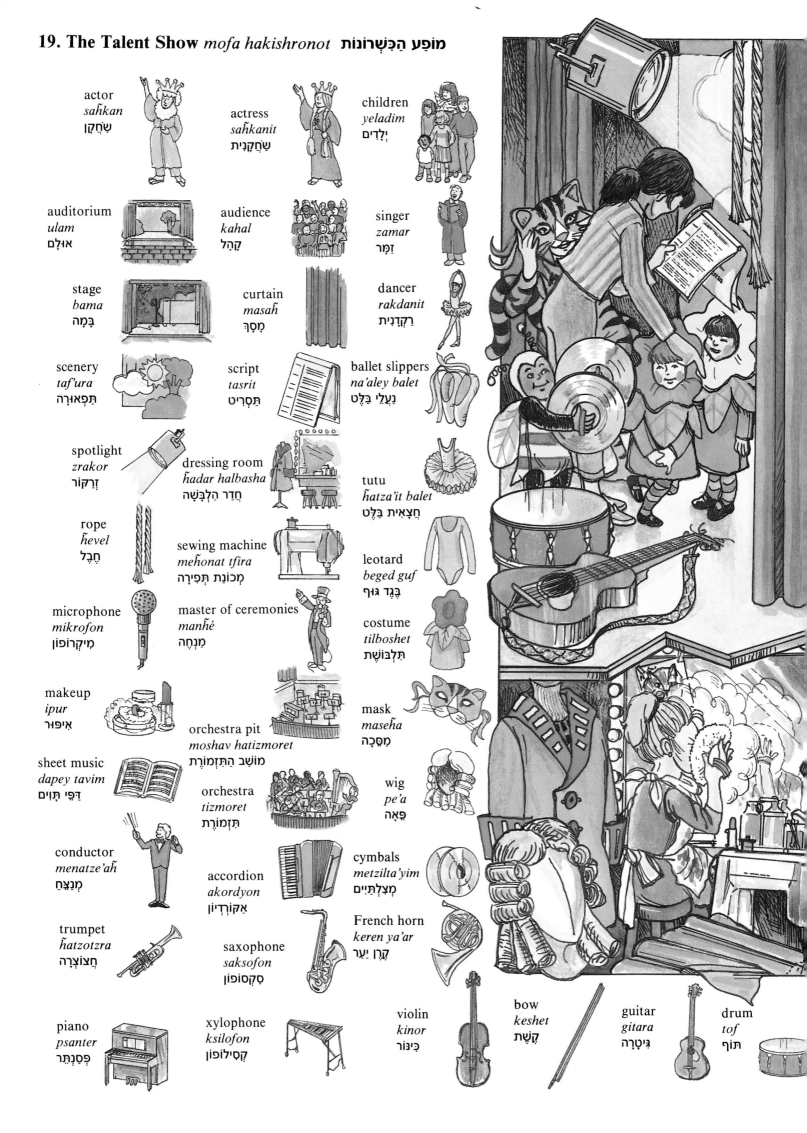

tuba
tuba
טוּבָּה

flute
ȟalil
חָלִיל

trombone
trombon
טְרוֹמְבּוֹן

clarinet
klarinet
קְלָרִינֶט

cello
chelo
צֶ'לוֹ

strings
meytarim
מֵיתָרִים

harp
nevel
נֵבֶל

20. At the Zoo *began haĥa'yot* בְּגַן הַחַיּוֹת

zookeeper
metapel
מְטַפֵּל

rhinoceros
karnaf
קַרְנַף

lion
aryé
אַרְיֵה

tiger
namer
נָמֵר

tiger cub
gur nemerim
גּוּר נְמֵרִים

jaguar
yagu'ar
יָגוּאָר

leopard
bardelas
בַּרְדְּלָס

flamingo
flamingo
פְלָמִינְגוֹ

owl
yanshuf
יַנְשׁוּף

swan
barbur
בַּרְבּוּר

penguin
pingwin
פִּינְגְוִוין

peacock
tavas
טַוָּס

eagle
a'yit
עַיִט

elephant
pil
פִּיל

ostrich
ya'en
יָעֵן

bear
dov
דּוֹב

bear cub
dubon
דּוּבּוֹן

polar bear
dov kotev
דּוֹב קוֹטֶב

panda
panda
פַּנְדָּה

gorilla
gorila
גּוֹרִילָה

parrot
tuki
תּוּכִּי

snake
naĥash
נָחָשׁ

seal
kelev yam
כֶּלֶב יָם

walrus
ari ha'yam
אֲרִי הַיָּם

hump
dabeshet
דַּבֶּשֶׁת

camel
gamal
גָּמָל

animals
ba'aley ĥa'yim
בַּעֲלֵי-חַיִּים

fox
shu'al
שׁוּעָל

wolf
ze'ev
זְאֵב

alligator
tanin
תַּנִּין

zebra
zebra
זֶבְּרָה

giraffe
jirafa
ג'ִירָפָה

monkey
kof
קוֹף

hippopotamus
hipopotam
הִיפּוֹפּוֹטָם

kangaroo
kenguru
קֶנְגוּרוּ

deer
tzvi
צְבִי

lizard
leta'a
לְטָאָה

turtle
tzav
צָב

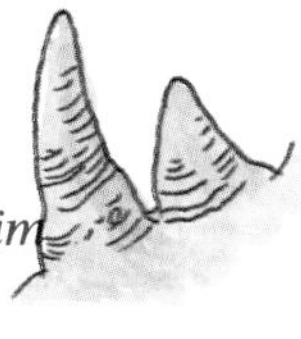
horns
karna'yim
קַרְנַיִם

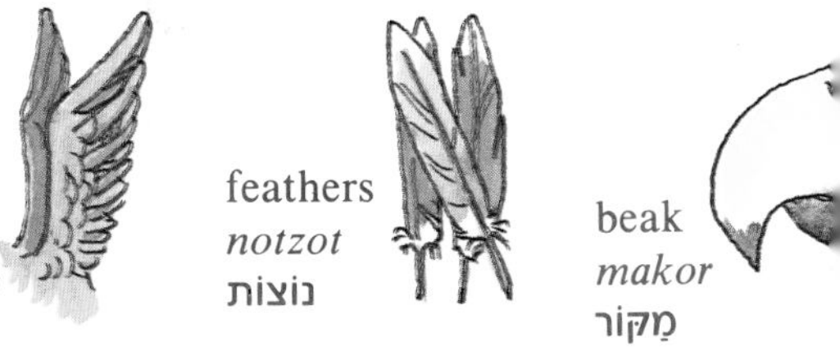
wings
knafa'yim
כְּנָפַיִים

feathers
notzot
נוֹצוֹת

beak
makor
מַקּוֹר

claws
tfarim
טְפָרִים

mane
ra'ama
רַעְמָה

tail
zanav
זָנָב

hoof
parsa
פַּרְסָה

stripes
pasim
פַּסִּים

spots
h̆avarburot
חֲבַרְבּוּרוֹת

21. At the Circus *bakirkas* בַּקִּרְקָס

clown
leytzan
לֵיצָן

popcorn
popkorn
פּוֹפְּקוֹרְן

caramel apple
tapu'aḥ mesukar
תַּפּוּחַ מְסוּכָּר

balloon
balon
בָּלוֹן

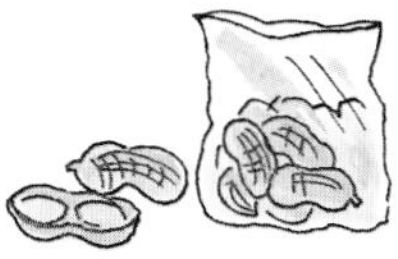

peanuts
boṭnim
בּוֹטְנִים

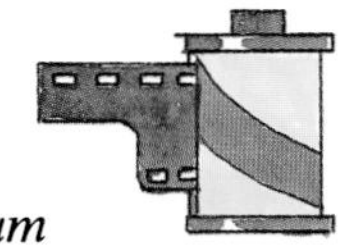

film
seret tzilum
סֶרֶט צִילּוּם

magician
kosem
קוֹסֵם

lion
aryé
אַרְיֵה

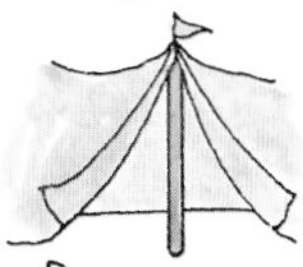

tent pole
mot merkazi
מוֹט מֶרְכָּזִי

elephant
pil
פִּיל

flashbulb
nurat flesh
נוּרַת פְלֶשׁ

camera
matzlema
מַצְלֵמָה

juggler
lahatutan
לַהֲטוּטָן

tickets
kartisim
כַּרְטִיסִים

baton
sharvit
שַׁרְבִיט

turban
turban
טוּרְבָּן

light bulb
nura
נוּרָה

night
layla
לַיְלָה

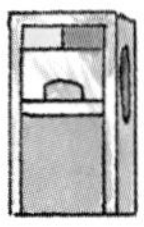

ticket booth
kupa
קוּפָּה

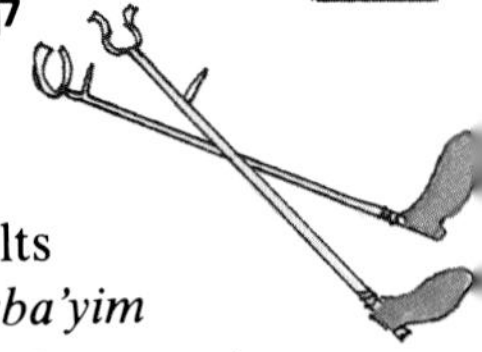

stilts
kaba'yim
קַבַּיִים

big top
ha'ohel
hamerkazi
הָאוֹהֶל הַמֶּרְכָּזִי

circus parade
mitz'ad hakirkas
מִצְעַד הַקִּרְקָס

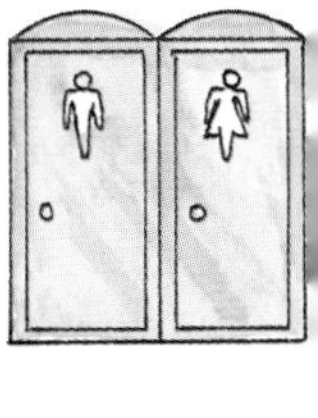

rest rooms
sherutim
שֵׁרוּתִים

bareback rider
lahatutan rehiva
לַהֲטוּטַן רְכִיבָה

tightrope walker
lulyanit al hevel
לוּלְיָינִית עַל חֶבֶל

tightrope
hevel lulyanim
חֶבֶל לוּלְיָינִים

handstand
amidat yada'yim
עֲמִידַת יָדַיִים

headstand
amidat rosh
עֲמִידַת רֹאשׁ

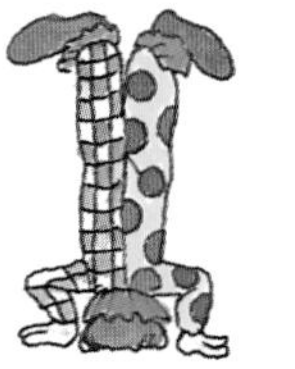

trapeze
trapez
טְרַפֶּז

trapeze artist
oman trapez
אָמַן טְרַפֶּז

acrobat
lulyan
לוּלְיָן

somersault
salta
סַלְטָה

cage
kluv
כְּלוּב

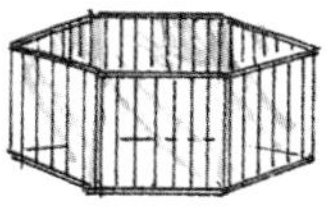

ring
zira
זִירָה

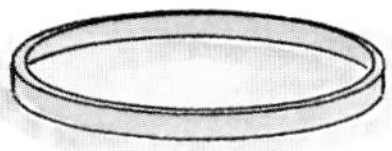

cartwheel
galgilon
גַּלְגִּילוֹן

safety net
reshet bitahon
רֶשֶׁת בִּיטָּחוֹן

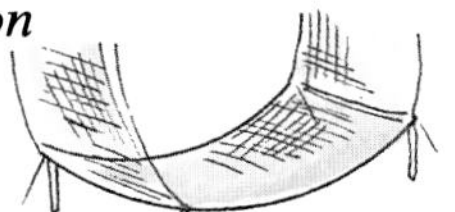

hoop
hishuk
חִישׁוּק

cotton candy
tzemer gefen matok
צֶמֶר גֶּפֶן מָתוֹק

band
tizmoret
תִּזְמוֹרֶת

whip
shot
שׁוֹט

rope ladder
sulam havalim
סוּלַּם חֲבָלִים

cape
glima
גְּלִימָה

lion tamer
me'alef ara'yot
מְאַלֵּף אֲרָיוֹת

unicycle
had ofan
חַד אוֹפַן

rope
hevel
חֶבֶל

ringmaster
manhé
מַנְחֶה

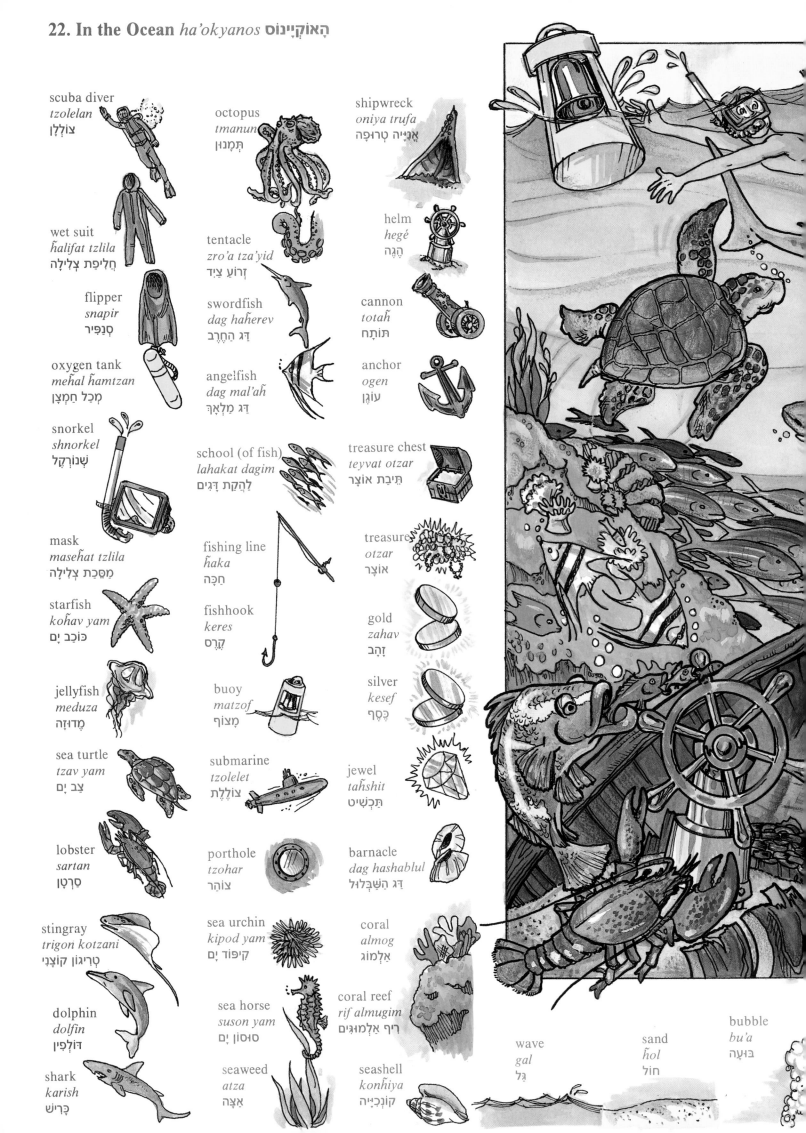

22. In the Ocean *ha'okyanos* הָאוֹקְיָינוֹס

scuba diver
tzolelan
צוֹלְלָן

wet suit
ĥalifat tzlila
חֲלִיפַת צְלִילָה

flipper
snapir
סְנַפִּיר

oxygen tank
meĥal ĥamtzan
מְכַל חַמְצָן

snorkel
shnorkel
שְׁנוֹרְקֶל

mask
maseĥat tzlila
מַסֵּכַת צְלִילָה

starfish
koĥav yam
כּוֹכַב יָם

jellyfish
meduza
מֶדוּזָה

sea turtle
tzav yam
צַב יָם

lobster
sartan
סַרְטָן

stingray
trigon kotzani
טְרִיגוֹן קוֹצָנִי

dolphin
dolfin
דּוֹלְפִין

shark
karish
כָּרִישׁ

octopus
tmanun
תְּמָנוּן

tentacle
zro'a tza'yid
זְרוֹעַ צַיִד

swordfish
dag haĥerev
דַּג הַחֶרֶב

angelfish
dag mal'aĥ
דַּג מַלְאָךְ

school (of fish)
lahakat dagim
לַהֲקַת דָּגִים

fishing line
ĥaka
חַכָּה

fishhook
keres
קֶרֶס

buoy
matzof
מָצוֹף

submarine
tzolelet
צוֹלֶלֶת

porthole
tzohar
צוֹהַר

sea urchin
kipod yam
קִיפּוֹד יָם

sea horse
suson yam
סוּסוֹן יָם

seaweed
atza
אַצָּה

shipwreck
oniya trufa
אֳנִיָּיה טְרוּפָה

helm
hegé
הֶגֶה

cannon
totaĥ
תּוֹתָח

anchor
ogen
עוֹגֶן

treasure chest
teyvat otzar
תֵּיבַת אוֹצָר

treasure
otzar
אוֹצָר

gold
zahav
זָהָב

silver
kesef
כֶּסֶף

jewel
taĥshit
תַּכְשִׁיט

barnacle
dag hashablul
דַּג הַשַּׁבְּלוּל

coral
almog
אַלְמוֹג

coral reef
rif almugim
רִיף אַלְמוּגִים

seashell
konĥiya
קוֹנְכִיָּיה

wave
gal
גַּל

sand
ĥol
חוֹל

bubble
bu'a
בּוּעָה

bareback rider
lahatutan reħiva
לַהֲטוּטַן רְכִיבָה

tightrope walker
lulyanit al ħevel
לוּלְיָינִית עַל חֶבֶל

tightrope
ħevel lulyanim
חֶבֶל לוּלְיָינִים

handstand
amidat yada'yim
עֲמִידַת יָדַיִים

headstand
amidat rosh
עֲמִידַת רֹאשׁ

trapeze
trapez
טְרַפֶּז

acrobat
lulyan
לוּלְיָן

somersault
salta
סַלְטָה

trapeze artist
oman trapez
אָמַּן טְרַפֶּז

cage
kluv
כְּלוּב

ring
zira
זִירָה

cartwheel
galgilon
גַּלְגִּילוֹן

safety net
reshet bitaħon
רֶשֶׁת בִּיטָּחוֹן

hoop
ħishuk
חִישׁוּק

cotton candy
tzemer gefen matok
צֶמֶר גֶּפֶן מָתוֹק

band
tizmoret
תִּזְמוֹרֶת

whip
shot
שׁוֹט

rope ladder
sulam ħavalim
סוּלַּם חֲבָלִים

cape
glima
גְּלִימָה

lion tamer
me'alef ara'yot
מְאַלֵּף אֲרָיוֹת

unicycle
ħad ofan
חַד אוֹפַן

rope
ħevel
חֶבֶל

ringmaster
manħé
מַנְחֶה

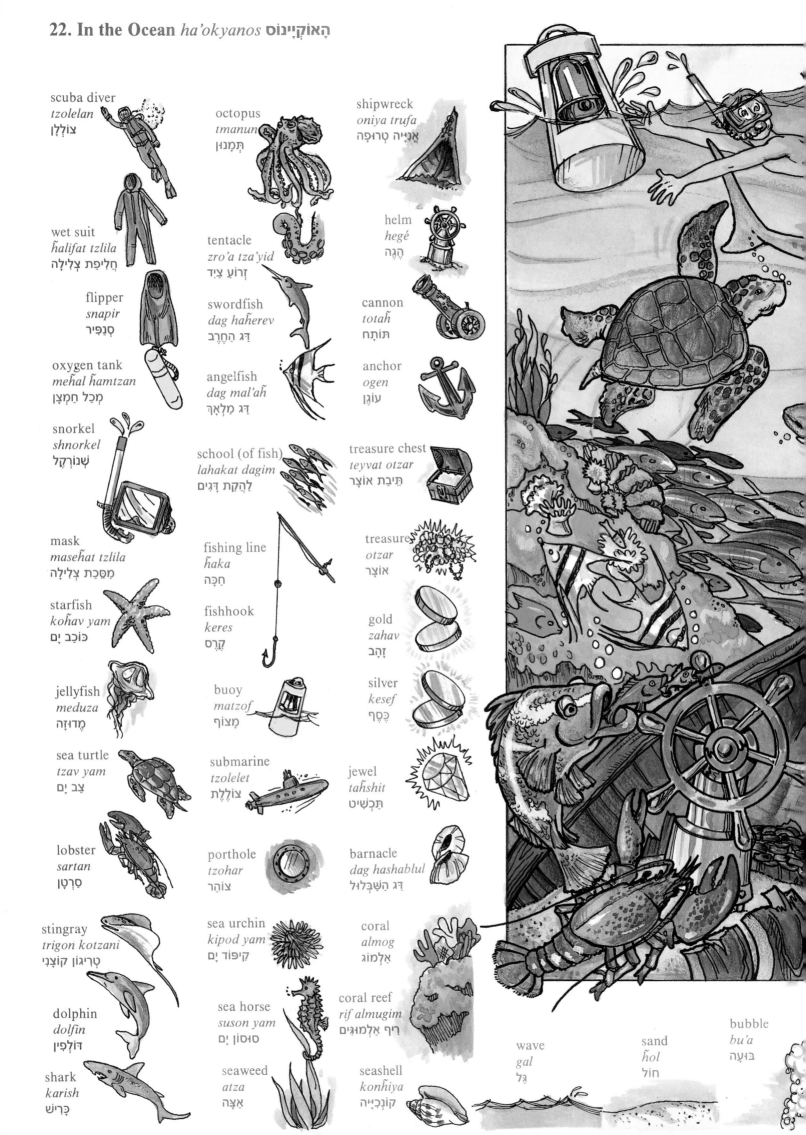

22. In the Ocean *ha'okyanos* הָאוֹקְיָינוֹס

scuba diver
tzolelan
צוֹלְלָן

wet suit
h̃alifat tzlila
חֲלִיפַת צְלִילָה

flipper
snapir
סְנַפִּיר

oxygen tank
meh̃al h̃amtzan
מְכַל חַמְצָן

snorkel
shnorkel
שְׁנוֹרְקֶל

mask
maseh̃at tzlila
מַסֵּכַת צְלִילָה

starfish
koh̃av yam
כּוֹכַב יָם

jellyfish
meduza
מֶדוּזָה

sea turtle
tzav yam
צַב יָם

lobster
sartan
סַרְטָן

stingray
trigon kotzani
טְרִיגוֹן קוֹצָנִי

dolphin
dolfin
דּוֹלְפִין

shark
karish
כָּרִישׁ

octopus
tmanun
תְּמָנוּן

tentacle
zro'a tza'yid
זְרוֹעַ צַיִד

swordfish
dag hah̃erev
דַּג הַחֶרֶב

angelfish
dag mal'ah̃
דַּג מַלְאָךְ

school (of fish)
lahakat dagim
לַהֲקַת דָּגִים

fishing line
h̃aka
חַכָּה

fishhook
keres
קֶרֶס

buoy
matzof
מָצוֹף

submarine
tzolelet
צוֹלֶלֶת

porthole
tzohar
צוֹהַר

sea urchin
kipod yam
קִיפּוֹד יָם

sea horse
suson yam
סוּסוֹן יָם

seaweed
atza
אַצָּה

shipwreck
oniya trufa
אֳנִיָּה טְרוּפָה

helm
hegé
הֶגֶה

cannon
totah̃
תּוֹתָח

anchor
ogen
עוֹגֶן

treasure chest
teyvat otzar
תֵּיבַת אוֹצָר

treasure
otzar
אוֹצָר

gold
zahav
זָהָב

silver
kesef
כֶּסֶף

jewel
tah̃shit
תַּכְשִׁיט

barnacle
dag hashablul
דַּג הַשַּׁבְּלוּל

coral
almog
אַלְמוֹג

coral reef
rif almugim
רִיף אַלְמוּגִּים

seashell
konh̃iya
קוֹנְכִיָּה

wave
gal
גַּל

sand
h̃ol
חוֹל

bubble
bu'a
בּוּעָה

cales
askasim
קַשְׂקַשִׂ

gills
zimim
זִימִים

fin
snapir
סְנַפִּיר

clam
tzidpa
צִדְפָּה

crab
sartan
סַרְטָן

squid
dyonun
דְּיוֹנוּן

whale
livyatan
לִוְויָתָן

23. Space *beĥalal* בֶּחָלָל

astronaut
ish ĥalal
אִישׁ חָלָל

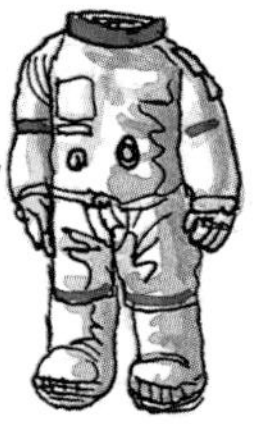

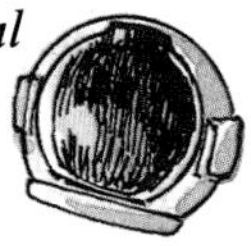

footprint
tvi'at regel
טְבִיעַת רֶגֶל

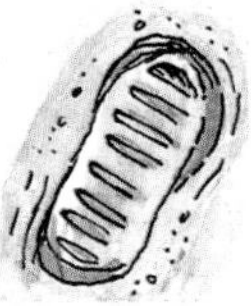

space shuttle
ma'aboret ĥalal
מַעְבּוֹרֶת חָלָל

cargo bay
shetaĥ mit'an
שֶׁטַח מִטְעָן

control panel
lu'aĥ bakara
לוּחַ בַּקָּרָה

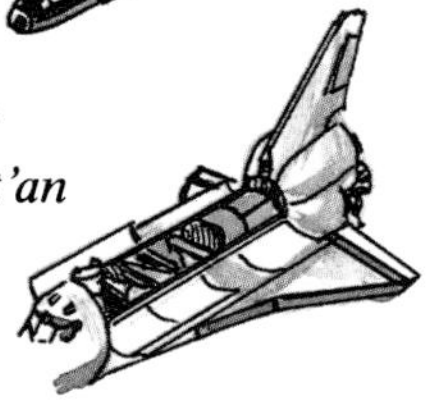

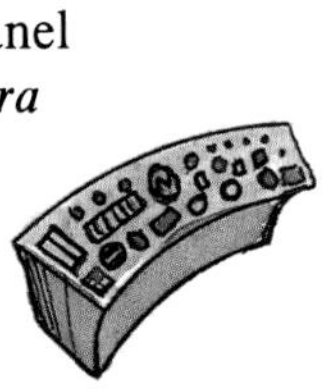

satellite
lavyan
לַוְיָן

spaceship
ĥalalit
חָלָלִית

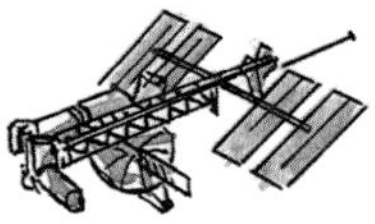

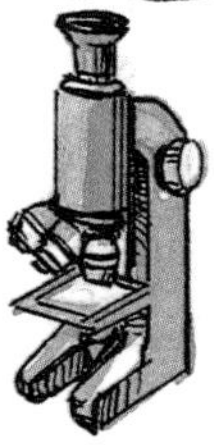

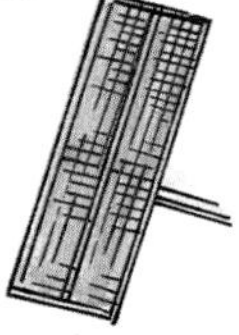

alien
yetzur me'olam aĥer
יְצוּר מֵעוֹלָם אַחֵר

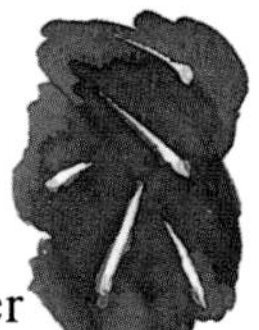

antenna
antena
אַנְטֶנָה

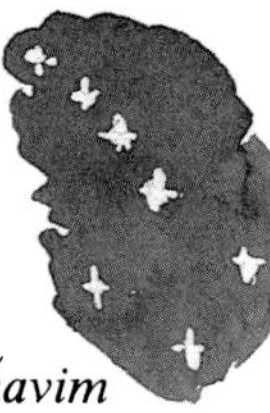

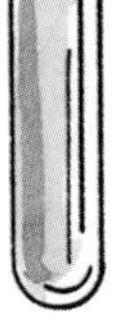

asteroid
astro'id
אַסְטְרוֹאִיד
space suit
ĥalifat ĥalal
חֲלִיפַת חָלָל

space walk
haliĥa baĥalal
הֲלִיכָה בֶּחָלָל

lunar rover
reĥev ĥalal
רֶכֶב חָלָל

landing capsule
ta neĥita
תָּא נְחִיתָה

ladder
sulam
סֻלָּם

space station
taĥanat ĥalal
תַּחֲנַת חָלָל

solar panel
lu'aĥ solari
לוּחַ סוֹלָרִי

meteor shower
metar mete'orim
מְטַר מֶטֶאוֹרִים

constellation
ma'areĥet koĥavim
מַעֲרֶכֶת כּוֹכָבִים

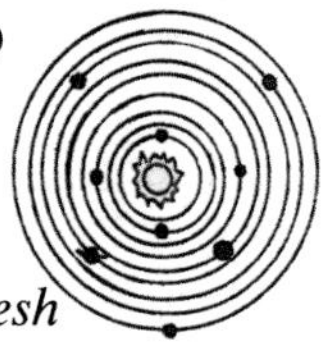

solar system
ma'areĥet shemesh
מַעֲרֶכֶת שֶׁמֶשׁ

space helmet
kasdat ĥalal
קַסְדַּת חָלָל

moon rock
sela yare'aĥ
סֶלַע יָרֵחַ

laboratory
ma'abada
מַעְבָּדָה

scientist
mad'an
מַדְעָן

lab coat
ĥaluk ma'abada
חָלוּק מַעְבָּדָה

microscope
mikroskop
מִיקְרוֹסְקוֹפּ

computer
maĥshev
מַחְשֵׁב

beaker
kli ma'abada
כְּלִי מַעְבָּדָה

test tube
mavĥena
מַבְחֵנָה

galaxy
galaksya
גָּלַקְסְיָה

earth
kadur ha'aretz
כַּדּוּר הָאָרֶץ

moon
yare'aĥ
יָרֵחַ

sun
shemesh
שֶׁמֶשׁ

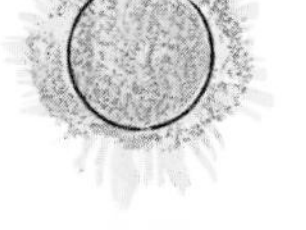

planet
koħav leħet
כּוֹכַב לֶכֶת

rings
taba'ot
טַבָּעוֹת

crater
maħtesh
מַכְתֵּשׁ

stars
koħavim
כּוֹכָבִים

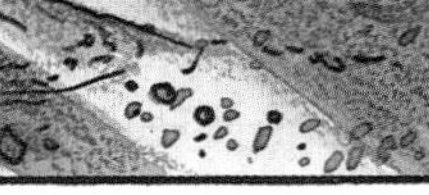

comet
koħav shavit
כּוֹכַב שָׁבִיט

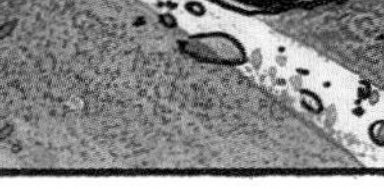

nebula
arfilit
עַרְפִילִית

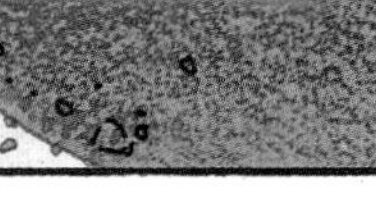

rocket
raketa
רַקֶטָה

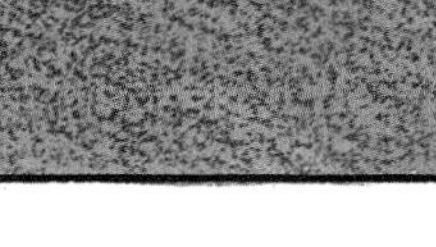

robot
robot
רוֹבּוֹט

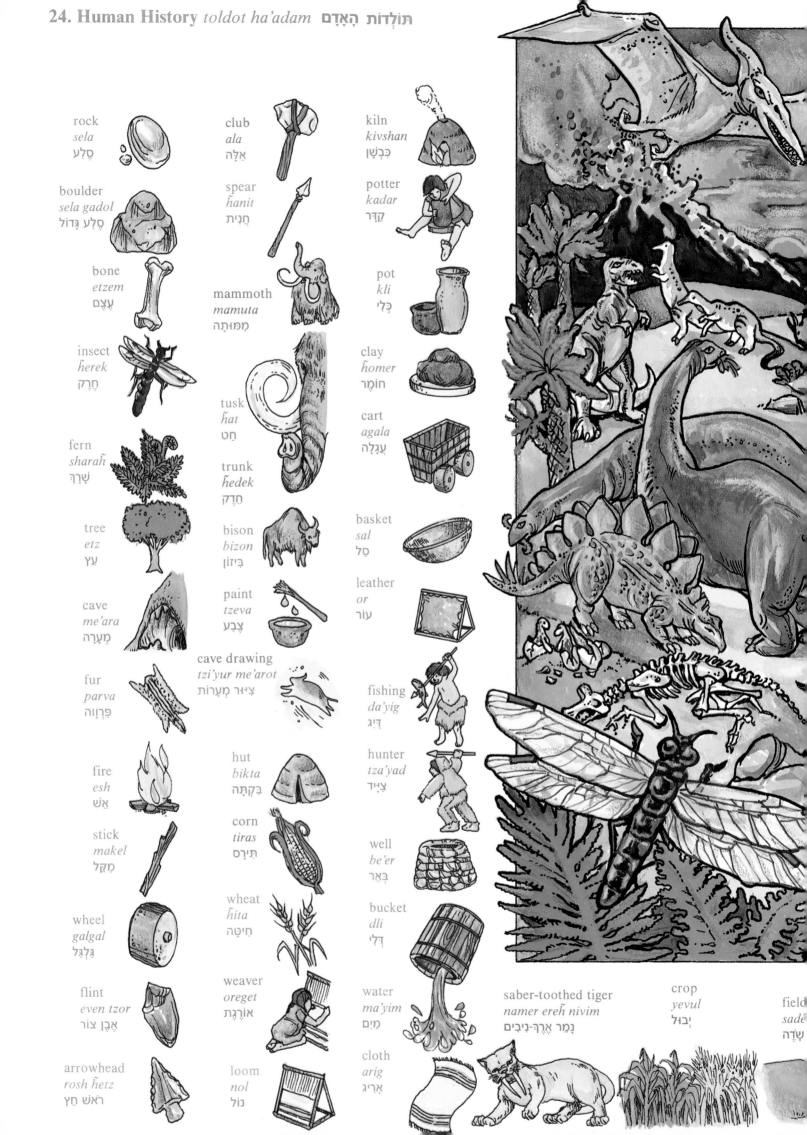

rock
sela
סֶלַע

boulder
sela gadol
סֶלַע גָּדוֹל

bone
etzem
עֶצֶם

insect
ĥerek
חֶרֶק

fern
sharaĥ
שָׁרָךְ

tree
etz
עֵץ

cave
me'ara
מְעָרָה

fur
parva
פַּרְוָוה

fire
esh
אֵשׁ

stick
makel
מַקֵּל

wheel
galgal
גַּלְגַּל

flint
even tzor
אֶבֶן צוֹר

arrowhead
rosh ĥetz
רֹאשׁ חֵץ

club
ala
אַלָּה

spear
ĥanit
חֲנִית

mammoth
mamuta
מָמוּתָה

tusk
ĥat
חַט

trunk
ĥedek
חֶדֶק

bison
bizon
בִּיזוֹן

paint
tzeva
צֶבַע

cave drawing
tzi'yur me'arot
צִיּוּר מְעָרוֹת

hut
bikta
בִּקְתָּה

corn
tiras
תִּירָס

wheat
ĥita
חִיטָּה

weaver
oreget
אוֹרֶגֶת

loom
nol
נוֹל

kiln
kivshan
כִּבְשָׁן

potter
kadar
קַדָּר

pot
kli
כְּלִי

clay
ĥomer
חוֹמֶר

cart
agala
עֲגָלָה

basket
sal
סַל

leather
or
עוֹר

fishing
da'yig
דַּיִּג

hunter
tza'yad
צַיָּד

well
be'er
בְּאֵר

bucket
dli
דְּלִי

water
ma'yim
מַיִם

cloth
arig
אָרִיג

saber-toothed tiger
namer ereĥ nivim
נָמֵר אֶרֶךְ-נִיבִים

crop
yevul
יְבוּל

field
sadê
שָׂדֶה

village
kfar
כְּפָר

cave dwellers
shoh̃ney me'arot
שׁוֹכְנֵי מְעָרוֹת

skeleton
sheled
שֶׁלֶד

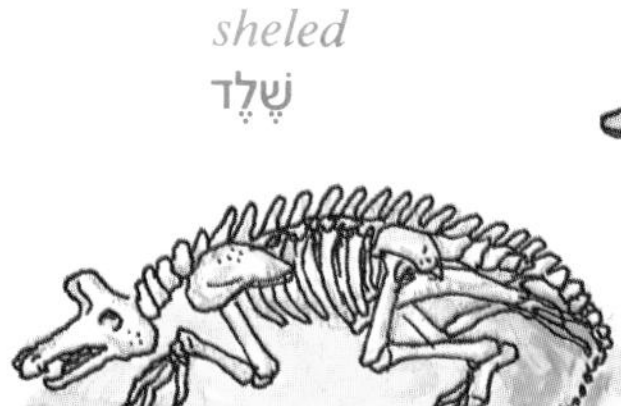

dinosaur
dinoza'ur
דִּינוֹזָאוּר

pterodactyl
leta'a me'ofefet
לְטָאָה מְעוֹפֶפֶת

25. The Make-Believe Castle *tirat ha'agadot* טִירַת הָאַגָּדוֹת

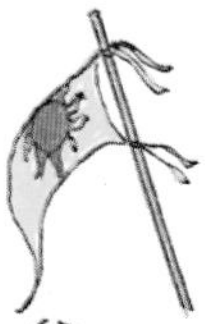
banner
degel
דֶּגֶל

dragon
drakon
דְּרָקוֹן

magic wand
maté ksamim
מַטֵּה קְסָמִים

fairy
fe'ya
פֵיָה

elf
shedon
שֵׁדוֹן

giant
anak
עֲנָק

forge
napaĥiya
נַפָּחִיָּיה

blacksmith
napaĥ
נַפָּח

anvil
sadan
סַדָּן

horseshoe
parsa
פַּרְסָה

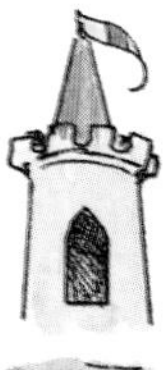
tower
migdal
מִגְדָּל

courtyard
ĥatzer
חָצֵר

squire
ben levaya
בֶּן לְוָיָה

knight
abir
אַבִּיר

armor
shiryon
שִׁרְיוֹן

chain mail
shiryon kaskasim
שִׁרְיוֹן קַשְׂקַשִּׂים

forest
ya'ar
יַעַר

saddle
ukaf
אוּכָּף

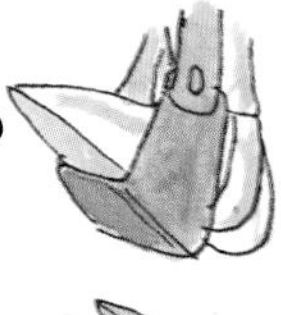
stirrup
arkof
אַרְכּוֹף

reins
resen
רֶסֶן

stable
urva
אוּרְוָה

dungeon
tzinok
צִינוֹק

moat
ĥafir magen
חֲפִיר מָגֵן

castle
tira
טִירָה

court jester
leytzan ĥatzer
לֵיצַן חָצֵר

minstrel
zamar noded
זַמָּר נוֹדֵד

unicorn
ĥad keren
חַד קֶרֶן

lance
romaĥ
רוֹמַח

shield
magen
מָגֵן

ax
garzen
גַּרְזֶן

sword
ĥerev
חֶרֶב

bow
keshet
קֶשֶׁת

arrow
ĥetz
חֵץ

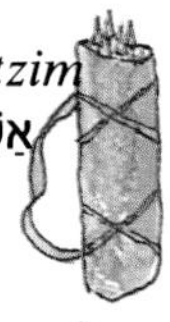
quiver
ashpat ĥitzim
אַשְׁפַּת חִצִּים

archer
kashat
קַשָּׁת

drawbridge
gesher niftaĥ
גֶּשֶׁר נִפְתָּח

bat
atalef
עֲטַלֵּף

rat
ĥulda
חוּלְדָּה

crown
keter
כֶּתֶר

king
meleȟ
מֶלֶךְ

queen
malka
מַלְכָּה

princess
nesiȟa
נְסִיכָה

prince
nasiȟ
נָסִיךְ

throne
kes malȟut
כֵּס מַלְכוּת

spider
akavish
עַכָּבִישׁ

spiderweb
kurey akavish
קוּרֵי עַכָּבִישׁ

26. The Mouse Hunt (Prepositions and Adjectives)

be'ikvot ha'aħbar (milot yaħas ut'arim) **בְּעִקְבוֹת הָעַכְבָּר (מִלּוֹת יַחַס וְתְאָרִים)**

up
lema'ala
לְמַעְלָה
sharp
ḥad
חַד
hot
ḥam
חַם
far
raḥok
רָחוֹק
fast
mahir
מָהִיר
cold
kar
קַר
top
elyon
עֶלְיוֹן
dull
kehé
קֵהֶה
down
lemata
לְמַטָּה
slow
iti
אִיטִי
old
yashan
יָשָׁן
left
smol
שְׂמֹאל
right
yamin
יָמִין
hard
kashé
קָשֶׁה
bottom
taḥton
תַּחְתּוֹן
new
ḥadash
חָדָשׁ
clean
naki
נָקִי
dirty
meluḥlaḥ
מְלוּכְלָךְ
light
kal
קַל
closed
sagur
סָגוּר
open
patu'aḥ
פָּתוּחַ
light
bahir
easy
kal
קַל
dark
kehé
כֵּהֶה
long
aroḥ
אָרוֹךְ
happy
same'aḥ
שָׂמֵחַ
sad
atzuv
עָצוּב
on
dolek
דּוֹלֵק
off
meḥubé
מְכוּבֶּה
thin
razé
רָזֶה
short
katzar
קָצָר
near
karov
קָרוֹב
between
beyn
בֵּין

27. Action Words *pe'ulot* פְּעוּלוֹת

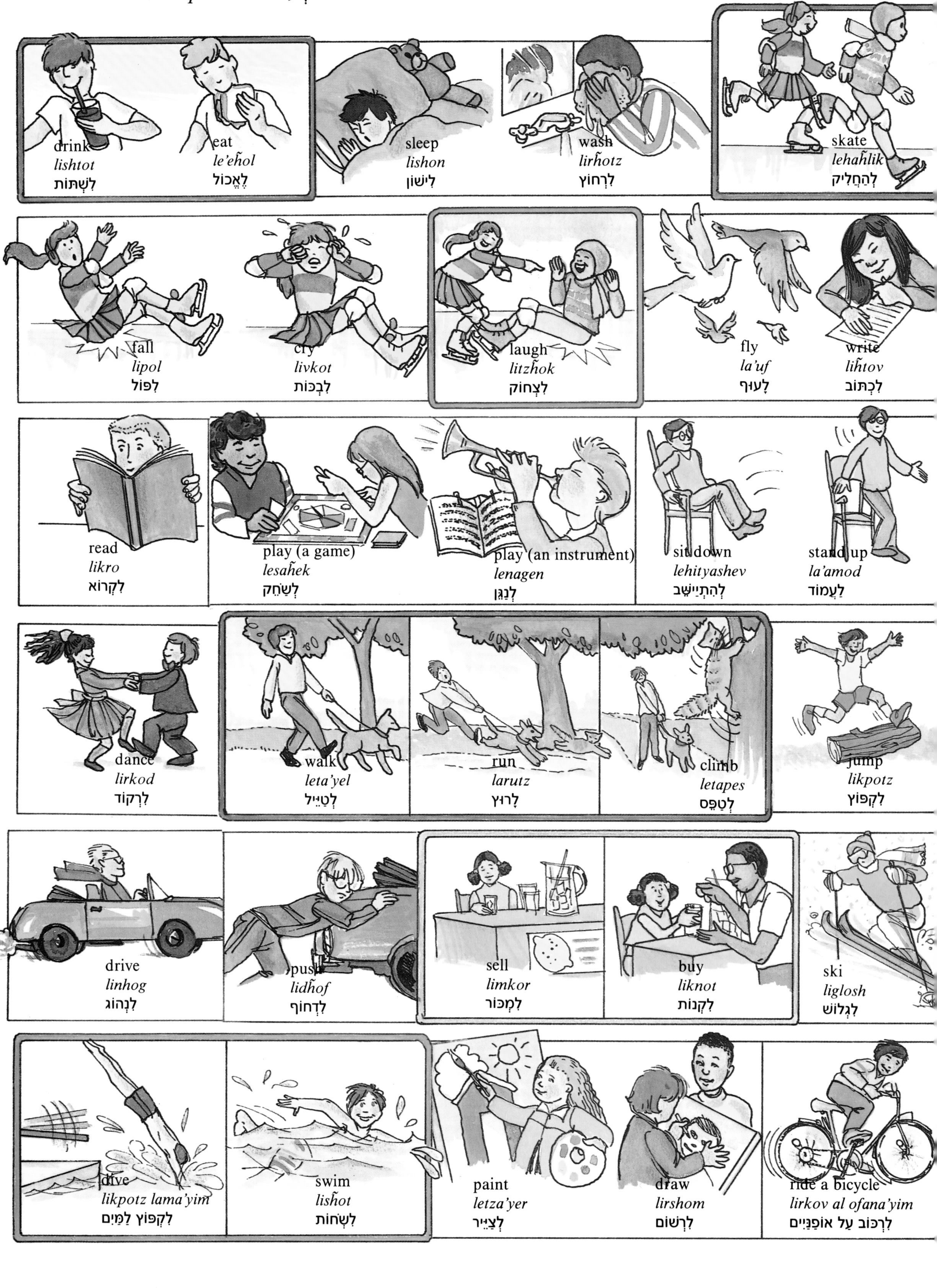
drink
lishtot
לִשְׁתּוֹת
eat
le'eȟol
לֶאֱכוֹל
sleep
lishon
לִישׁוֹן
wash
lirȟotz
לִרְחוֹץ
skate
lehaȟlik
לְהַחֲלִיק
fall
lipol
לִפּוֹל
cry
livkot
לִבְכּוֹת
laugh
litzȟok
לִצְחוֹק
fly
la'uf
לָעוּף
write
liȟtov
לִכְתּוֹב
read
likro
לִקְרוֹא
play (a game)
lesaȟek
לְשַׂחֵק
play (an instrument)
lenagen
לְנַגֵּן
sit down
lehityashev
לְהִתְיַישֵּׁב
stand up
la'amod
לַעֲמוֹד
dance
lirkod
לִרְקוֹד
walk
leta'yel
לְטַיֵּיל
run
larutz
לָרוּץ
climb
letapes
לְטַפֵּס
jump
likpotz
לִקְפּוֹץ
drive
linhog
לִנְהוֹג
push
lidȟof
לִדְחוֹף
sell
limkor
לִמְכּוֹר
buy
liknot
לִקְנוֹת
ski
liglosh
לִגְלוֹשׁ
dive
likpotz lama'yim
לִקְפּוֹץ לַמַּיִם
swim
lisȟot
לִשְׂחוֹת
paint
letza'yer
לְצַיֵּיר
draw
lirshom
לִרְשׁוֹם
ride a bicycle
lirkov al ofana'yim
לִרְכּוֹב עַל אוֹפַנַּיִם

come
lavo
לָבוֹא
go
laleĥet
לָלֶכֶת
throw
lizrok
לִזְרוֹק
catch
litpos
לִתְפּוֹס
watch
lehistakel
לְהִסְתַּכֵּל
sing
lashir
לָשִׁיר
talk
ledaber
לְדַבֵּר
kick
liv'ot
לִבְעוֹט
listen (to)
lehakshiv
לְהַקְשִׁיב
think
laĥshov
לַחְשׁוֹב
roar
lish'og
לִשְׁאוֹג
dig
laĥpor
לַחְפּוֹר
pour
lishpoĥ
לִשְׁפּוֹךְ
juggle
lelahatet
לְלַהֲטֵט
point (at)
lehatzbi'a
לְהַצְבִּיעַ
look for
leĥapes
לְחַפֵּשׂ
find
limtzo
לִמְצוֹא
give
latet
לָתֵת
receive
lekabel
לְקַבֵּל
cut
ligzor
לִגְזוֹר
cook
levashel
לְבַשֵּׁל
open
lifto'aĥ
לִפְתּוֹחַ
close
lisgor
לִסְגּוֹר
take a bath
lehitraĥetz
לְהִתְרַחֵץ
teach
lelamed
לְלַמֵּד
break
lishbor
לִשְׁבּוֹר
fix
letaken
לְתַקֵּן
carry
lisĥov
לִסְחוֹב
pull
limshoĥ
לִמְשׁוֹךְ
wait
leĥakot
לְחַכּוֹת

28. Colors *tzva'im* צְבָעִים

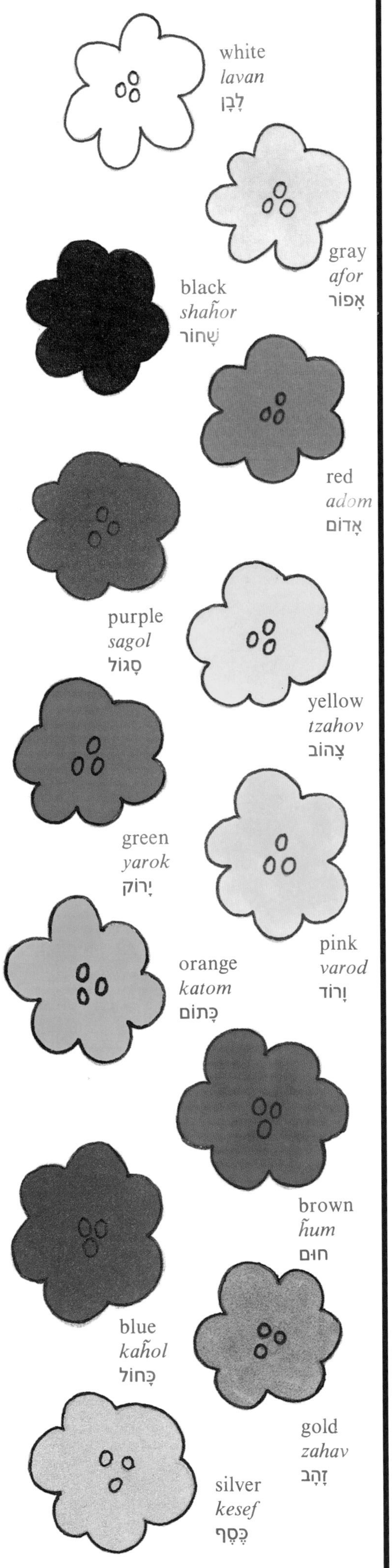

29. The Family Tree *ilan hamishpaĥa* אִילַן הַמִּשְׁפָּחָה

grandfather, grandpa
saba
סַבָּא

uncle
dod
דּוֹד

aunt
doda
דּוֹדָה

cousin
ben dod
בֶּן-דּוֹד

cousin
bat doda
בַּת-דּוֹדָה

daughter
bat
בַּת

30. Shapes *tzurot* צוּרוֹת

square
ribu'a
רִיבּוּעַ

triangle
meshulash
מְשׁוּלָּשׁ

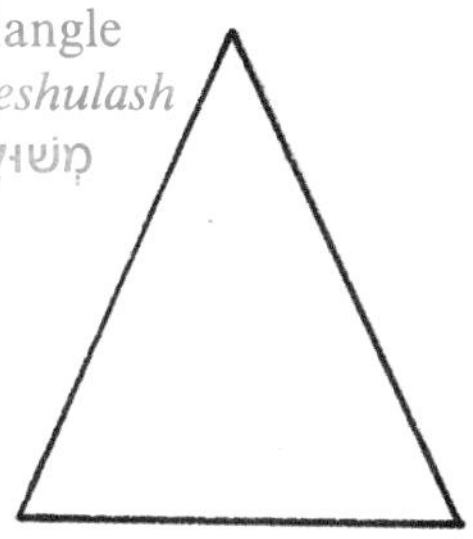

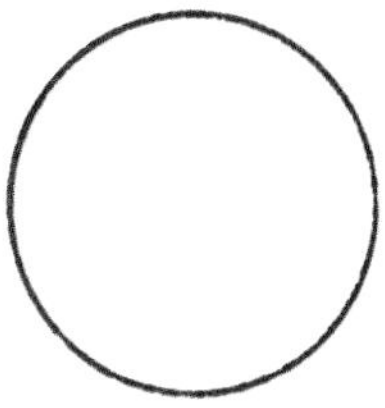

circle
ma'agal
מַעְגָּל

rectangle
malben
מַלְבֵּן

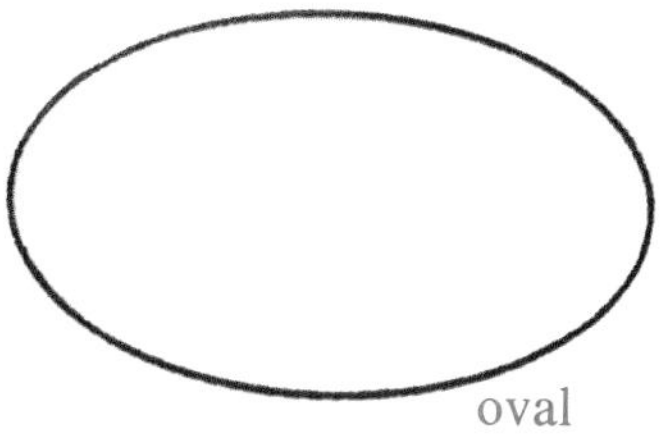

oval
elipsa
אֶלִיפְּסָה

cube
kubiya
קוּבִּיָּה

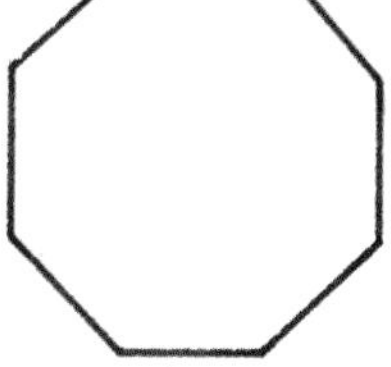

octagon
metuman
מְתוּמָּן

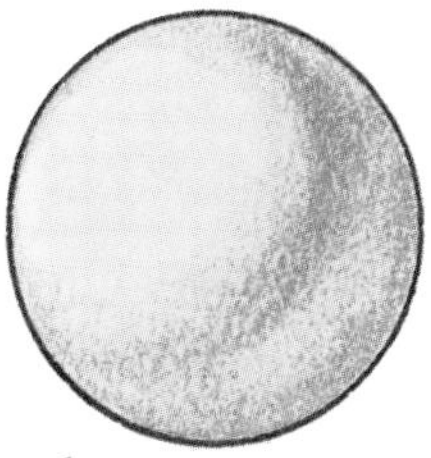

sphere
kadur
כַּדּוּר

cylinder
galil
גָּלִיל

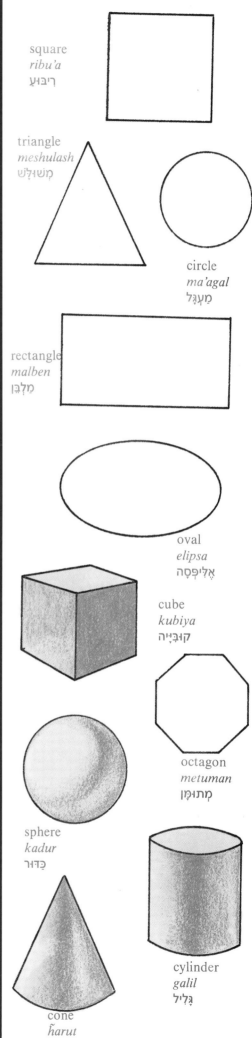

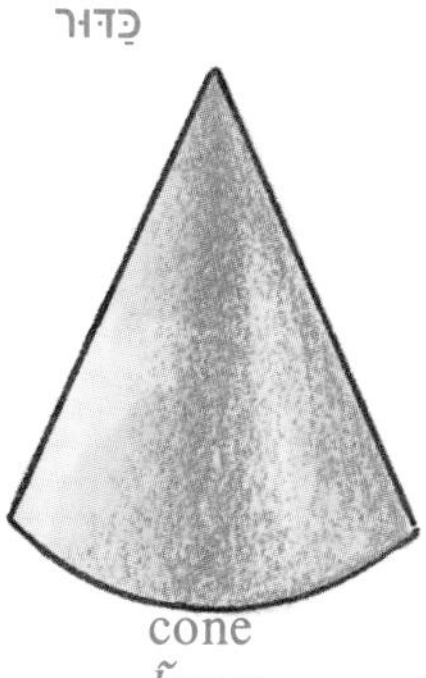

cone
ħarut
חָרוּט

31. Numbers *misparim* מִסְפָּרִים

Ordinal Numbers
misparim siduri'yim
מִסְפָּרִים סִידּוּרִיִּים

tenth	*asiri*	עֲשִׂירִי
ninth	*tshi'i*	תְּשִׁיעִי
eighth	*shmini*	שְׁמִינִי
seventh	*shvi'i*	שְׁבִיעִי
sixth	*shishi*	שִׁישִּׁי
fifth	*ȟamishi*	חֲמִישִּׁי
fourth	*revi'i*	רְבִיעִי
third	*shlishi*	שְׁלִישִׁי
second	*sheni*	שֵׁנִי
first	*rishon*	רִאשׁוֹן

Cardinal Numbers
misparim yesodi'yim
מִסְפָּרִים יְסוֹדִיִּים

0	zero	*efes*	אֶפֶס
½	half	*ȟatzi*	חֲצִי
1	one	*eȟat*	אַחַת
2	two	*shta'yim*	שְׁתַּיִם
3	three	*shalosh*	שָׁלוֹשׁ
4	four	*arba*	אַרְבַּע
5	five	*ȟamesh*	חָמֵשׁ
6	six	*shesh*	שֵׁשׁ
16	sixteen	*shesh esré*	שֵׁשׁ-עֶשְׂרֵה
17	seventeen	*shva esré*	שְׁבַע-עֶשְׂרֵה
18	eighteen	*shmoné esré*	שְׁמוֹנֶה-עֶשְׂרֵה
19	nineteen	*tsha esré*	תְּשַׁע-עֶשְׂרֵה
20	twenty	*esrim*	עֶשְׂרִים
21	twenty-one	*esrim ve'aȟat*	עֶשְׂרִים וְאַחַת
28	twenty-eight	*esrim ushmoné*	עֶשְׂרִים וּשְׁמוֹנֶה
29	twenty-nine	*esrim va tesha*	עֶשְׂרִים וָתֵשַׁע
30	thirty	*shloshim*	שְׁלוֹשִׁים
31	thirty-one	*shloshim ve'aȟat*	שְׁלוֹשִׁים וְאַחַת
37	thirty-seven	*shloshim va sheva*	שְׁלוֹשִׁים וָשֶׁבַע
38	thirty-eight	*shloshim ushmoné*	שְׁלוֹשִׁים וּשְׁמוֹנֶה
39	thirty-nine	*shloshim va tesha*	שְׁלוֹשִׁים וָתֵשַׁע
40	forty	*arba'im*	אַרְבָּעִים
46	forty-six	*arba'im va shesh*	אַרְבָּעִים וָשֵׁשׁ
47	forty-seven	*arba'im va sheva*	אַרְבָּעִים וָשֶׁבַע
48	forty-eight	*arba'im ushmoné*	אַרְבָּעִים וּשְׁמוֹנֶה
49	forty-nine	*arba'im va tesha*	אַרְבָּעִים וָתֵשַׁע
55	fifty-five	*ȟamishim ve'ȟamesh*	חֲמִישִּׁים וְחָמֵשׁ
56	fifty-six	*ȟamishim va shesh*	חֲמִישִּׁים וָשֵׁשׁ
57	fifty-seven	*ȟamishim va sheva*	חֲמִישִּׁים וָשֶׁבַע
58	fifty-eight	*ȟamishim ushmoné*	חֲמִישִּׁים וּשְׁמוֹנֶה
64	sixty-four	*shishim ve'arba*	שִׁישִּׁים וְאַרְבַּע
65	sixty-five	*shishim ve'ȟamesh*	שִׁישִּׁים וְחָמֵשׁ
66	sixty-six	*shishim va shesh*	שִׁישִּׁים וָשֵׁשׁ
67	sixty-seven	*shishim va sheva*	שִׁישִּׁים וָשֶׁבַע
73	seventy-three	*shiv'im ve'shalosh*	שִׁבְעִים וְשָׁלוֹשׁ
74	seventy-four	*shiv'im ve'arba*	שִׁבְעִים וְאַרְבַּע
75	seventy-five	*shiv'im ve'ȟamesh*	שִׁבְעִים וְחָמֵשׁ
76	seventy-six	*shiv'im va shesh*	שִׁבְעִים וָשֵׁשׁ
82	eighty-two	*shmonim ushta'yim*	שְׁמוֹנִים וּשְׁתַּיִם
83	eighty-three	*shmonim ve'shalosh*	שְׁמוֹנִים וְשָׁלוֹשׁ
84	eighty-four	*shmonim ve'arba*	שְׁמוֹנִים וְאַרְבַּע
85	eighty-five	*shmonim ve'ȟamesh*	שְׁמוֹנִים וְחָמֵשׁ
91	ninety-one	*tish'im ve'aȟat*	תִּשְׁעִים וְאַחַת
92	ninety-two	*tish'im ushta'yim*	תִּשְׁעִים וּשְׁתַּיִם
93	ninety-three	*tish'im ve'shalosh*	תִּשְׁעִים וְשָׁלוֹשׁ
94	ninety-four	*tish'im ve'arba*	תִּשְׁעִים וְאַרְבַּע
100	hundred	*me'a*	מֵאָה
1,000	thousand	*elef*	אֶלֶף
10,000	ten thousand	*aseret alafim*	עֲשֶׂרֶת אֲלָפִים

7
seven
sheva
שֶׁבַע

8
eight
shmoné
שְׁמוֹנֶה

9
nine
tesha
תֵּשַׁע

10
ten
eser
עֶשֶׂר

11
eleven
ahat esré
אַחַת-עֶשְׂרֵה

12
twelve
shtem esré
שְׁתֵּים-עֶשְׂרֵה

13
thirteen
shlosh esré
שְׁלוֹשׁ-עֶשְׂרֵה

14
fourteen
arba esré
אַרְבַּע-עֶשְׂרֵה

15
fifteen
hamesh esré
חֲמֵשׁ-עֶשְׂרֵה

22
twenty-two
esrim ushta'yim
עֶשְׂרִים וּשְׁתַּיִים

23
twenty-three
esrim ve'shalosh
עֶשְׂרִים וְשָׁלוֹשׁ

24
twenty-four
esrim ve'arba
עֶשְׂרִים וְאַרְבַּע

25
twenty-five
esrim ve'hamesh
עֶשְׂרִים וְחָמֵשׁ

26
twenty-six
esrim va shesh
עֶשְׂרִים וָשֵׁשׁ

27
twenty-seven
esrim va sheva
עֶשְׂרִים וָשֶׁבַע

32
thirty-two
shloshim ushta'yim
שְׁלוֹשִׁים וּשְׁתַּיִים

33
thirty-three
shloshim ve'shalosh
שְׁלוֹשִׁים וְשָׁלוֹשׁ

34
thirty-four
shloshim ve'arba
שְׁלוֹשִׁים וְאַרְבַּע

35
thirty-five
shloshim ve'hamesh
שְׁלוֹשִׁים וְחָמֵשׁ

36
thirty-six
shloshim va shesh
שְׁלוֹשִׁים וָשֵׁשׁ

41
forty-one
arba'im ve'ahat
אַרְבָּעִים וְאַחַת

42
forty-two
arba'im ushta'yim
אַרְבָּעִים וּשְׁתַּיִים

43
forty-three
arba'im ve'shalosh
אַרְבָּעִים וְשָׁלוֹשׁ

44
forty-four
arba'im ve'arba
אַרְבָּעִים וְאַרְבַּע

45
forty-five
arba'im ve'hamesh
אַרְבָּעִים וְחָמֵשׁ

50
fifty
hamishim
חֲמִישִּׁים

51
fifty-one
hamishim ve'ahat
חֲמִישִּׁים וְאַחַת

52
fifty-two
hamishim ushta'yim
חֲמִישִּׁים וּשְׁתַּיִים

53
fifty-three
hamishim ve'shalosh
חֲמִישִּׁים וְשָׁלוֹשׁ

54
fifty-four
hamishim ve'arba
חֲמִישִּׁים וְאַרְבַּע

59
fifty-nine
hamishim va tesha
חֲמִישִּׁים וָתֵשַׁע

60
sixty
shishim
שִׁישִּׁים

61
sixty-one
shishim ve'ahat
שִׁישִּׁים וְאַחַת

62
sixty-two
shishim ushta'yim
שִׁישִּׁים וּשְׁתַּיִים

63
sixty-three
shishim ve'shalosh
שִׁישִּׁים וְשָׁלוֹשׁ

68
sixty-eight
shishim ushmoné
שִׁישִּׁים וּשְׁמוֹנֶה

69
sixty-nine
shishim va tesha
שִׁישִּׁים וָתֵשַׁע

70
seventy
shiv'im
שִׁבְעִים

71
seventy-one
shiv'im ve'ahat
שִׁבְעִים וְאַחַת

72
seventy-two
shiv'im ushta'yim
שִׁבְעִים וּשְׁתַּיִים

77
seventy-seven
shiv'im va sheva
שִׁבְעִים וָשֶׁבַע

78
seventy-eight
shiv'im ushmoné
שִׁבְעִים וּשְׁמוֹנֶה

79
seventy-nine
shiv'im va tesha
שִׁבְעִים וָתֵשַׁע

80
eighty
shmonim
שְׁמוֹנִים

81
eighty-one
shmonim ve'ahat
שְׁמוֹנִים וְאַחַת

86
eighty-six
shmonim va shesh
שְׁמוֹנִים וָשֵׁשׁ

87
eighty-seven
shmonim va sheva
שְׁמוֹנִים וָשֶׁבַע

88
eighty-eight
shmonim ushmoné
שְׁמוֹנִים וּשְׁמוֹנֶה

89
eighty-nine
shmonim va tesha
שְׁמוֹנִים וָתֵשַׁע

90
ninety
tish'im
תִּשְׁעִים

95
ninety-five
tish'im ve'hamesh
תִּשְׁעִים וְחָמֵשׁ

96
ninety-six
tish'im va shesh
תִּשְׁעִים וָשֵׁשׁ

97
ninety-seven
tish'im va sheva
תִּשְׁעִים וָשֶׁבַע

98
ninety-eight
tish'im ushmoné
תִּשְׁעִים וּשְׁמוֹנֶה

99
ninety-nine
tish'im va tesha
תִּשְׁעִים וָתֵשַׁע

00,000
hundred thousand
me'a elef
מֵאָה אֶלֶף

1,000,000
million
milyon
מִילְיוֹן

1,000,000,000
billion
milyard
מִילְיַארְד

32. A Map of the World *mapat ha'olam* מַפַּת הָעוֹלָם

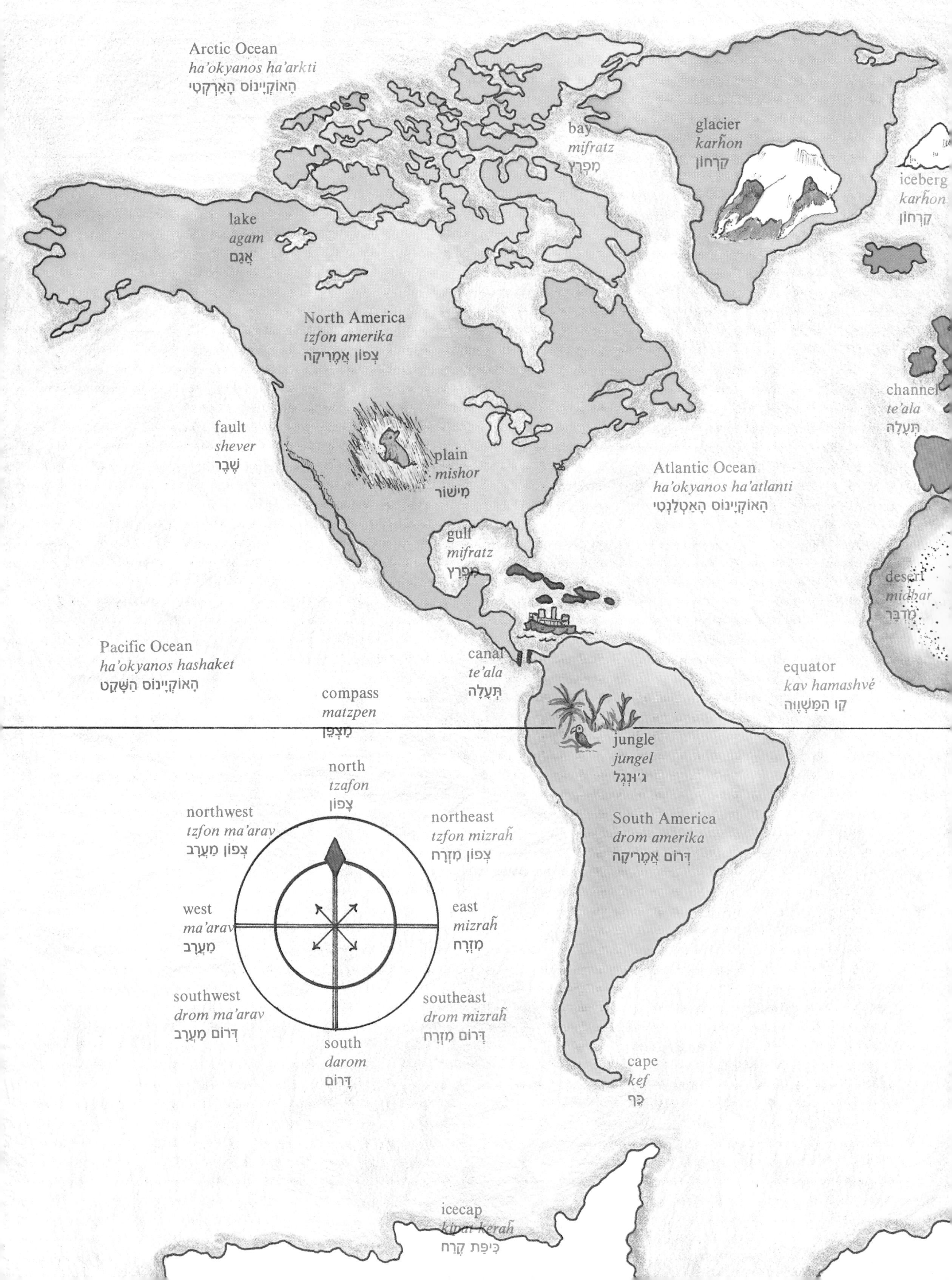
Arctic Ocean
ha'okyanos ha'arkti
הָאוֹקְיָינוֹס הָאַרְקְטִי
bay
mifratz
מִפְרָץ
glacier
karhon
קַרְחוֹן
iceberg
karhon
קַרְחוֹן
lake
agam
אֲגַם
North America
tzfon amerika
צְפוֹן אֲמֶרִיקָה
channel
te'ala
תְּעָלָה
fault
shever
שֶׁבֶר
plain
mishor
מִישׁוֹר
Atlantic Ocean
ha'okyanos ha'atlanti
הָאוֹקְיָינוֹס הָאַטְלַנְטִי
gulf
mifratz
מִפְרָץ
desert
midbar
מִדְבָּר
Pacific Ocean
ha'okyanos hashaket
הָאוֹקְיָינוֹס הַשָּׁקֵט
canal
te'ala
תְּעָלָה
equator
kav hamashvé
קַו הַמַּשְׁוֶה
compass
matzpen
מַצְפֵּן
jungle
jungel
ג'וּנְגֶל
north
tzafon
צָפוֹן
northwest
tzfon ma'arav
צְפוֹן מַעֲרָב
northeast
tzfon mizrah
צְפוֹן מִזְרָח
South America
drom amerika
דְּרוֹם אֲמֶרִיקָה
west
ma'arav
מַעֲרָב
east
mizrah
מִזְרָח
southwest
drom ma'arav
דְּרוֹם מַעֲרָב
southeast
drom mizrah
דְּרוֹם מִזְרָח
south
darom
דָּרוֹם
cape
kef
כֵּף
icecap
kipat kerah
כִּיפַּת קֶרַח

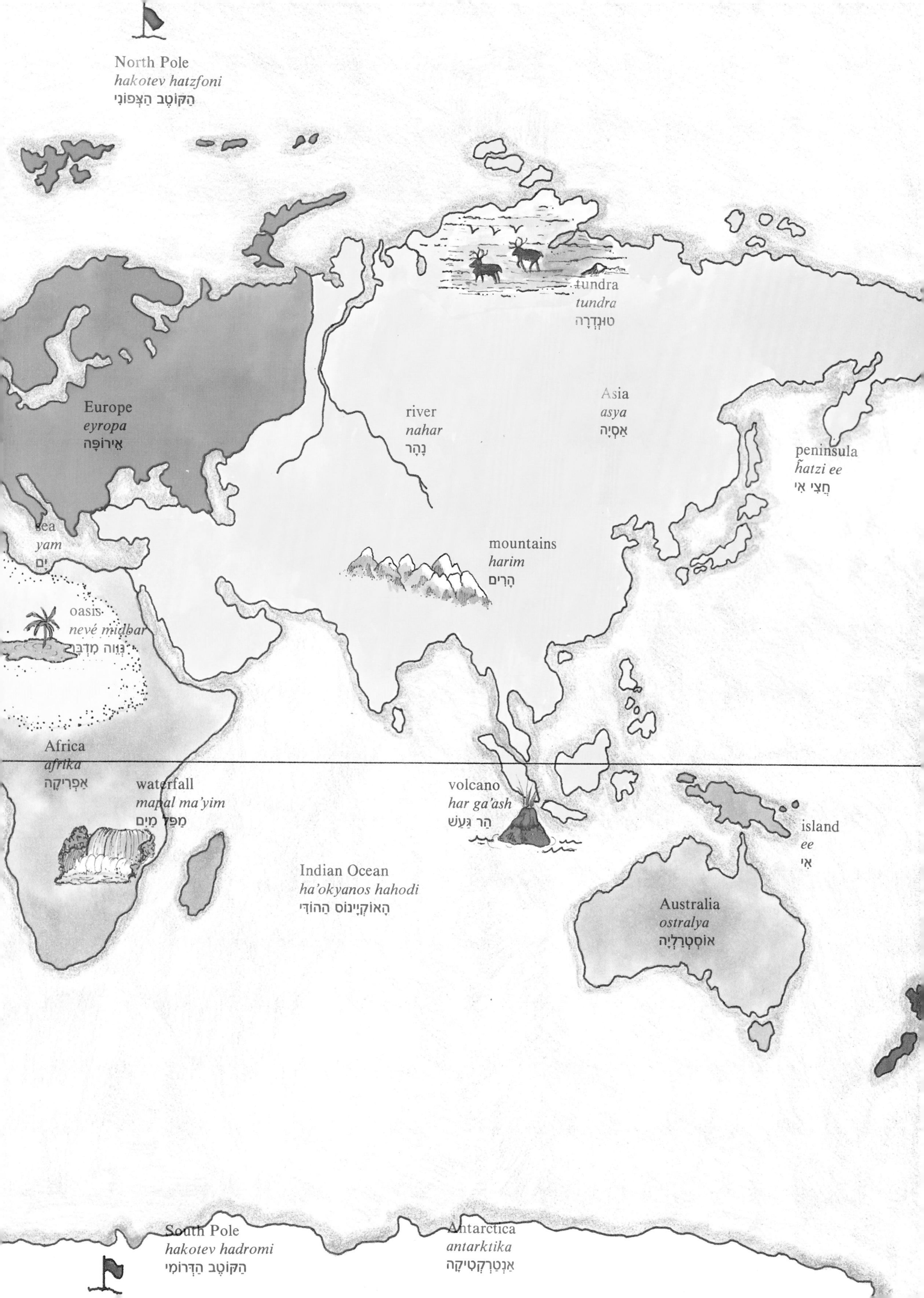

North Pole
hakotev hatzfoni
הַקּוֹטֶב הַצְּפוֹנִי
tundra
tundra
טוּנְדְּרָה
Europe
eyropa
אֵירוֹפָּה
river
nahar
נָהָר
Asia
asya
אַסְיָה
peninsula
ħatzi ee
חֲצִי אִי
sea
yam
יָם
mountains
harim
הָרִים
oasis
nevé midbar
נְוֵה מִדְבָּר
Africa
afrika
אַפְרִיקָה
waterfall
mapal ma'yim
מַפַּל מַיִם
volcano
har ga'ash
הַר גַּעַשׁ
island
ee
אִי
Indian Ocean
ha'okyanos hahodi
הָאוֹקְיָינוֹס הַהוֹדִי
Australia
ostralya
אוֹסְטְרַלְיָה
South Pole
hakotev hadromi
הַקּוֹטֶב הַדְּרוֹמִי
Antarctica
antarktika
אַנְטַרְקְטִיקָה

Hebrew-English Glossary and Index

Note: the sign h̄, which stands for the Hebrew sound /ח/, appears before the letter 'h'

da'yig / **fishing** 24
dabeshet / **hump** 20
dafdefet / **notepad** 13
dag / **fish** 1, 10
dag hah̃erev / **swordfish** 22
dag hashablul / **barnacle** 22
dag mal'ah̃ / **angelfish** 22
dalgit / **jump rope** 4
dam / **blood** 11
damka / **checkers** 4
dapey tavim / **sheet music** 19
darkon / **passport** 17
darom / **south** 32
davar / **postal worker** 13
davar / **letter carrier** 15
davsha / **pedal** 14
dayag / **fisherman** 15
dayal / **flight attendant** 17
degel / **banner** 25
delet / **door** 2
delpek / **counter** 3
delpek kartisim / **ticket counter** 17
dereh̃ / **road** 9
dereh̃ gisha / **driveway** 8
deshé / **grass** 9
devek / **glue** 1
dgalim / **flags** 17
dganim / **cereal** 6
dinoza'ur / **dinosaur** 24
dli / **bucket** 24
dod / **uncle** 29
doda / **aunt** 29
dolek / **on** 26
dolfin / **dolphin** 22
dov / **bear** 20
dov kotev / **polar bear** 20
drakon / **dragon** 25
drom amerika / **South America** 32
drom ma'arav / **southwest** 32
drom mizrah̃ / **southeast** 32
dubi / **teddy bear** 4
dubon / **bear cub** 20
dugmanit / **model** 15
duvdevanim / **cherries** 6
dvorim / **bees** 9
dyonun / **squid** 22

ee / **island** 32
efes / **zero** 31
efro'ah̃ / **chick** 9
efronot tziv'oniyim / **colored pencils** 1
egel / **calf** 9
eglat kniyot / **shopping cart** 6
eglat mit'an / **baggage cart** 17
eglat tinok / **baby carriage** 16
eglat tiyul / **stroller** 16
egozim / **nuts** 6
eh̃at / **one** 31
elef / **thousand** 31
elipsa / **oval** 30
elyon / **top** 26
eser / **ten** 31
esh / **fire** 24
eshkolit / **grapefruit** 6
esrim / **twenty** 31
esrim ushmoné / **twenty-eight** 31
esrim ushta'yim / **twenty-two** 31
esrim va shesh / **twenty-six** 31
esrim va sheva / **twenty-seven** 31
esrim va tesha / **twenty-nine** 31
esrim ve'ah̃at / **twenty-one** 31

esrim ve'arba / **twenty-four** 31
esrim ve'h̃amesh / **twenty-five** 31
esrim ve'shalosh / **twenty-three** 31
et / **shovel** 5
et / **pen** 1
etz / **tree** 24, 9
etz / **wood** 3
etzba / **toe** 11
etzba / **finger** 11
etzem / **bone** 24
even tzor / **flint** 24
eyna'yim / **eyes** 11
eyropa / **Europe** 32

fe'ya / **fairy** 25
flamingo / **flamingo** 20
futbol / **football** 18

gaba / **eyebrow** 11
gader / **fence** 9
gadol / **large** 26
gafrurim / **matches** 5
gag / **roof** 2
gag niftah̃ / **sunroof** 14
gal / **wave** 22
galaksya / **galaxy** 23
galay matah̃ot / **metal detector** 17
galgal / **wheel** 24
galgal tviya / **spinning wheel** 4
galgaley ezer / **training wheels** 14
galgiliyot / **roller skates** 16
galgilon / **cartwheel** 21
gali / **wavy** 12
galil / **cylinder** 30
galshan avir / **hang glider** 16
gamal / **camel** 20
gan / **park** 8
gan mish̃akim / **playground** 8
gan yarak / **vegetable garden** 5
ganan / **gardener** 15
garba'yim / **socks** 7
garbiyonim / **tights** 7
garzen / **ax** 25
gav / **back** 11
gavi'a / **trophy** 18
gavoha / **tall** 26
gdi / **kid** 9
geshem / **rain** 5
gesher / **braces** 11
gesher / **bridge** 16
gesher niftah̃ / **drawbridge** 25
gever / **man** 9
geves / **cast** 11
gezer / **carrots** 6
gir / **chalk** 1
gitara / **guitar** 19
giv'a / **hill** 9
giv'ol / **stem** 5
glida / **ice cream** 10
glima / **cape** 21
glisha / **downhill skiing** 18
globus / **globe** 1
gluya / **postcard** 13
golf / **golf** 18
gored sh̃hakim / **skyscraper** 8
gorila / **gorilla** 20
gulot / **marbles** 4
gumiya / **rubber band** 13
gur nemerim / **tiger cub** 20
gvina / **cheese** 6

h̃ad / **sharp** 26
h̃ad keren / **unicorn** 25
h̃ad ofan / **unicycle** 21
h̃adar ambatya / **bathroom** 2
h̃adar halbasha / **dressing room** 19
h̃adar hamtana / **waiting room** 11
h̃adar kasafot / **safe** 13
h̃adar megurim / **living room** 2
h̃adar oh̃el / **dining room** 2
h̃adar sheyna / **bedroom** 2
h̃adash / **new** 26
h̃afir magen / **moat** 25
h̃agav / **grasshopper** 5
h̃agora / **belt** 7
h̃agorat betih̃ut / **seat belt** 14
h̃aka / **fishing line** 22
h̃alak / **straight** 12
h̃alalit / **spaceship** 23
h̃alav / **milk** 6
h̃alifa / **suit** 7
h̃alifat h̃alal / **space suit** 23
h̃alifat tzlila / **wet suit** 22
h̃alil / **flute** 19
h̃alon / **window** 2
h̃alon kidmi / **windshield** 14
h̃aluk ma'abada / **lab coat** 23
h̃aluk rah̃atza / **bathrobe** 7
h̃am / **hot** 26
h̃amesh / **five** 31
h̃amesh esré / **fifteen** 31
h̃amishi / **fifth** 31
h̃amishim / **fifty** 31
h̃amishim ushmoné / **fifty-eight** 31
h̃amishim ushta'yim / **fifty-two** 31
h̃amishim va shesh / **fifty-six** 31
h̃amishim va sheva / **fifty-seven** 31
h̃amishim va tesha / **fifty-nine** 31
h̃amishim ve'ah̃at / **fifty-one** 31
h̃amishim ve'arba / **fifty-four** 31
h̃amishim ve'h̃amesh / **fifty-five** 31
h̃amishim ve'shalosh / **fifty-three** 31
h̃amor / **donkey** 9
h̃anit / **spear** 24
h̃anut bgadim / **clothing store** 8
h̃anut makolet / **grocery story** 8

madaf / **shelf** 2
mad'an / **scientist** 23
madħan / **parking meter** 8
madħef / **propeller** 17
madħom / **thermometer** 11
madim / **uniform** 4
madregot / **stairs** 2
madregot ħerum / **fire escape** 8
madregot na'ot / **escalator** 17
madriħat tiyulim / **tour guide** 15
mafte'aħ / **key** 13
mafte'aħ bragim / **wrench** 3
magafa'yim / **boots** 7
magash / **tray** 10
magbeha / **jack** 14
magen / **shield** 25
magevet / **towel** 2
magévim / **windshield wipers** 14
magfey bokrim / **cowboy boots** 4
maghetz / **iron** 3
maglesha / **slide** 8
magnet / **magnet** 4
magrefa / **rake** 5
magvot niyar / **paper towels** 3
maħavat / **pan** 3
maħbena / **barrette** 12
maħberet / **notebook** 1
maħbet / **racket** 18
maħbet tenis / **tennis racket** 17
maħbet zvuvim / **fly swatter** 5
maħlev / **stapler** 1
maħlika'yim / **skates** 18
maħog / **hand** 1
maħseħat deshé / **lawn mower** 5
maħshev / **computer** 23
maħshevon / **calculator** 1
maħshir vidyo / **videocassette player** 2
maħtesh / **crater** 23
maħzir or / **reflectors** 14
mahir / **fast** 26
makdeħa / **drill** 3
makel / **cane** 11
makel / **stick** 24
makor / **beak** 20
makrena / **movie projector** 4
malben / **rectangle** 30
malé / **full** 26
malka / **queen** 25
mamtakim / **candy** 6
mamtera / **sprinkler** 5
mamuta / **mammoth** 24
manħé / **ringmaster** 21
manħé / **master of ceremonies** 19
manikuristit / **manicurist** 12
mano'a / **engine** 17, 14
man'ul / **lock** 13
mapa / **map** 1
mapal ma'yim / **waterfall** 32
mapat shulħan / **tablecloth** 10
mapit / **napkin** 10
mar'a / **mirror** 2
mar'a aħorit / **rearview mirror** 14
marak / **soup** 10
marit / **spatula** 3
marpek / **elbow** 11
masaħ / **curtain** 19
masaħ makam / **radar screen** 17
masa'it / **truck** 16
masa'it grar / **tow truck** 14
maseħa / **mask** 19
maseħat tzlila / **mask** 22
mash'evat delek / **gas pump** 14
mashké kal / **soft drink** 10
mashot / **oar** 16
mashrokit / **whistle** 4
maskara / **mascara** 12
masket / **stethoscope** 11
maslul / **runway** 17
masmer / **nail** 3
maso'a mit'an / **baggage claim** 17
masok / **helicopter** 16
masor / **saw** 3
masregot / **knitting needles** 4
masrek / **comb** 12
matana / **gift** 10
mataté / **broom** 3
matbe'a / **coin** 13
maté ksamim / **magic wand** 25
matlé / **sling** 11
matos / **airplane** 17, 16
matzlema / **camera** 21, 17
matzlemat bitaħon / **security camera** 13
matzlemat vide'o / **video camera** 17
matzne'aħ / **parachute** 18
matznem / **toaster** 3
matzof / **buoy** 22
matzpen / **compass** 32
mavħena / **test tube** 23
mavreg / **screwdriver** 3
mazkira / **secretary** 15
mazleg / **fork** 10
mazrek / **hypodermic needle** 11
me'a / **hundred** 31
me'a elef / **hundred thousand** 31
me'abed mazon / **food processor** 3
me'aħor / **behind** 26
me'al / **above** 26
me'alef ara'yot / **lion tamer** 21
me'ara / **cave** 24
me'arbel beton / **cement mixer** 16
me'arbel ħashmali / **electric mixer** 3
me'atzevet ofna / **fashion designer** 15
me'atzevet se'ar / **hairstylist** 12
me'avrer / **fan** 5
medalya / **medal** 18
mediaħ kelim / **dishwasher** 3
meduza / **jellyfish** 22
mefaleset sheleg / **snowplow** 5
megera / **drawer** 3
meħaded / **pencil sharpener** 1
meħal ħamtzan / **oxygen tank** 22
meħalit / **tank truck** 14
meħamemey ozna'yim / **earmuffs** 7
meħir / **price** 6
meħonat ktiva / **typewriter** 13
meħonat kvisa / **washing machine** 3
meħonat tfira / **sewing machine** 19
meħonay / **mechanic** 14
meħonit / **car** 16
meħonit merotz / **race car** 14
meħorer / **hole punch** 1
meħubé / **off** 26
meħuga / **compass** 1
mehadek / **paper clip** 13
me'il / **coat** 7
me'il geshem / **raincoat** 7
mekarer / **refrigerator** 3
melaħ / **salt** 10
meleħ / **king** 25
melon / **melon** 6
meltzar / **waiter** 10
meltzarit / **waitress** 10
meluħlaħ / **dirty** 26
menahel avoda / **foreman** 15
menatze'aħ / **conductor** 19
menifa / **fan** 4
menora / **lamp** 2
merotz meħoniyot / **car racing** 18
merotz susim / **horse racing** 18
meshek / **farm** 9
meshulash / **triangle** 30
mesibat yom huledet / **birthday party** 10
mesuħot / **hurdles** 18
metaħnet maħshevim / **computer programmer** 15
metaltel / **curling iron** 12
metapel / **zookeeper** 20
metar mete'orim / **meteor shower** 23
meter / **tape measure** 3
metultal / **curly** 12
metuman / **octagon** 30
metupal / **patient** 11
metzaħ / **forehead** 11
metzilta'yim / **cymbals** 19
meyabesh kvisa / **clothes dryer** 3
meyabesh se'ar / **hair dryer** 12
meyabesh se'ar / **blow dryer** 12
meytarim / **strings** 19
meyza / **sweatshirt** 7
mezaħ / **dock** 16
midbar / **desert** 32
midraħa / **sidewalk** 16
mif'al / **factory** 8
mifras / **sail** 16
mifrasit / **sailboat** 16
mifratz / **bay** 32
mifratz / **gulf** 32
migdal / **tower** 25
migdal piku'aħ / **control tower** 17
migdalor / **lighthouse** 16
miglasha'yim / **skis** 18
miħnasa'yim / **pants** 7
miħnasa'yim ktzarim / **shorts** 7
miħnesey trening / **sweatpants** 7
miħsé delek / **gas cap** 14
miħsé hamano'a / **hood** 14

ratov / **wet** 26
razé / **thin** 26
regel / **leg** 11
reh̃ev h̃alal / **lunar rover** 23
reh̃iva al ofana'yim / **cycling** 18
reh̃iva al susim / **horseback riding** 18
rek / **empty** 26
resen / **reins** 25
reshamkol / **cassette player** 2
reshet / **net** 18
reshet bitah̃on / **safety net** 21
revi'i / **fourth** 31
riba / **jam** 10
ribu'a / **square** 30
rif almugim / **coral reef** 22
rishon / **first** 31
ritza / **running** 18
ritzpa / **floor** 2
robot / **robot** 23
rof'a / **doctor** 11
rofé shina'yim / **dentist** 11
roh̃san / **zipper** 7
rokah̃at / **pharmacist** 15
rolim / **curlers** 12
romah̃ / **lance** 25
rosh / **head** 11
rosh h̃etz / **arrowhead** 24
ru'ah̃ / **wind** 5

sa / **go!** 16
saba / **grandfather ,grandpa** 29
sabal / **porter** 17
sabal / **baggage handler** 17
sabon / **soap** 6
sadan / **anvil** 25
sadé / **field** 24
sadin / **sheet** 2
safam / **mustache** 12
safran / **librarian** 15
safsal / **bench** 8
sagol / **purple** 28
sagur / **closed** 26
sah̃kan / **actor** 19
sah̃kanit / **actress** 19
sak do'ar / **mailbag** 13
sak shena / **sleeping bag** 9
sakin / **knife** 10
sakit / **shopping bag** 6
saksofon / **saxophone** 19
sal / **basket** 24
sal ashpa / **wastebasket** 1
salat / **salad** 10
salta / **somersault** 21
same'ah̃ / **happy** 26
sandalim / **sandals** 7
santer / **chin** 11
sapa / **sofa** 2
sapar / **barber** 12
sarbal / **coveralls** 14
sargel / **ruler** 1
sartan / **crab** 22
sartan / **lobster** 22
savta / **grandmother ,grandma** 29
se'ar / **hair** 12
sefel / **cup** 10
sefer / **book** 1
sela / **rock** 24
sela gadol / **boulder** 24
sela yare'ah̃ / **moon rock** 23
seleri / **celery** 10
seret tzilum / **film** 21
sfata'yim / **lips** 11
sfaton / **lipstick** 12
sfina / **boat** 16
sfinat avir / **blimp** 16
sfinat grar / **tugboat** 16
sfog / **sponge** 3
sfog meh̃ika / **(chalkboard) eraser** 1
sh̃ah̃at metosim / **hangar** 17
sh̃ava al makel / **mop** 3
sh̃iya / **swimming** 18
sha'ar / **gate** 17
shah̃at / **hay** 9
shah̃mat / **chess** 4
shah̃or / **black** 12
shah̃or / **black** 28
shalosh / **three** 31
shama'yim / **sky** 9
shamen / **fat** 26
shamenet / **cream** 10
shampu / **shampoo** 12
sha'on / **clock** 1
sha'on me'orer / **alarm clock** 2
sharah̃ / **fern** 24
sharsheret / **necklace** 7
sharsheret / **bicycle chain** 14
sharvit / **baton** 21
sharvul / **sleeve** 7
shatiah̃ / **rug** 1
shatiah̃ / **carpet** 2
she'u'it yeruka / **green beans** 6
shedon / **elf** 25
sheka h̃ashmali / **electrical outlet** 3
sheled / **skeleton** 24
sheleg / **snow** 5
shelet / **sign** 8, 6
shemen / **oil** 14
shemesh / **sun** 23
shen / **tooth** 11
sheni / **second** 31
sherutim / **rest rooms** 21
shesh / **six** 31
shesh esré / **sixteen** 31
shetah̃ mit'an / **cargo bay** 23
sheva / **seven** 31
shever / **fault** 32
shida / **dresser** 2
shinanit / **dental hygienist** 11
shiryon / **armor** 25
shiryon kaskasim / **chain mail** 25
shishi / **sixth** 31
shishim / **sixty** 31
shishim ushmoné / **sixty-eight** 31
shishim ushta'yim / **sixty-two** 31
shishim va shesh / **sixty-six** 31
shishim va sheva / **sixty-seven** 31
shishim va tesha / **sixty-nine** 31
shishim ve'ah̃at / **sixty-one** 31
shishim ve'arba / **sixty-four** 31
shishim ve'h̃amesh / **sixty-five** 31
shishim ve'shalosh / **sixty-three** 31
shiv'im / **seventy** 31
shiv'im ushmoné / **seventy-eight** 31
shiv'im ushta'yim / **seventy-two** 31
shiv'im va shesh / **seventy-six** 31
shiv'im va sheva / **seventy-seven** 31
shiv'im va tesha / **seventy-nine** 31
shiv'im ve'ah̃at / **seventy-one** 31
shiv'im ve'arba / **seventy-four** 31
shiv'im ve'h̃amesh / **seventy-five** 31
shiv'im ve'shalosh / **seventy-three** 31
shlishi / **third** 31
shlosh esré / **thirteen** 31
shloshim / **thirty** 31
shloshim ushmoné / **thirty-eight** 31
shloshim ushta'yim / **thirty-two** 31
shloshim va shesh / **thirty-six** 31
shloshim va sheva / **thirty-seven** 31
shloshim va tesha / **thirty-nine** 31
shloshim ve'ah̃at / **thirty-one** 31
shloshim ve'arba / **thirty-four** 31
shloshim ve'h̃amesh / **thirty-five** 31
shloshim ve'shalosh / **thirty-three** 31
shlulit / **puddle** 5
shmini / **eighth** 31
shmoné / **eight** 31
shmoné esré / **eighteen** 31
shmonim / **eighty** 31
shmonim ushmoné / **eighty-eight** 31
shmonim ushta'yim / **eighty-two** 31
shmonim va shesh / **eighty-six** 31
shmonim va sheva / **eighty-seven** 31
shmonim va tesha / **eighty-nine** 31
shmonim ve'ah̃at / **eighty-one** 31
shmonim ve'arba / **eighty-four** 31
shmonim ve'h̃amesh / **eighty-five** 31
shmonim ve'shalosh / **eighty-three** 31
shnorkel / **snorkel** 22
sho'er / **doorman** 15
sho'ev avak / **vacuum cleaner** 3
shofet / **umpire** 18
shofet / **referee** 18
shofetet / **judge** 15
shoh̃ney me'arot / **cave dwellers** 24
shokolad / **chocolate** 6
sh'on yad / **watch** 7
shot / **whip** 21
shoter / **policeman** 15
shoteret / **policewoman** 15
shravrav / **plumber** 15
shta'yim / **two** 31
shtar / **bill** 13
shtem esré / **twelve** 31
shtifat meh̃oniyot / **car wash** 14
shu'al / **fox** 20
shulh̃an / **table** 3
shulh̃an bdika / **examining table** 11
shulh̃an hamora / **teacher's desk** 1
shulh̃an hatalmid / **pupil desk** 1

shulħan layla / **night table** 2
shva esré / **seventeen** 31
shvi'i / **seventh** 31
shvil / **part** 12
si'aħ / **bush** 5
sikot / **staples** 1
simla / **dress** 7
simlat neshef / **ball gown** 4
sinor / **apron** 3
sirat mano'a / **motorboat** 16
sirat meshotim / **rowboat** 16
sketbord / **skateboard** 16
smartut / **rag** 14
smiħa / **blanket** 2
smol / **left** 26
snapir / **fin** 22
snapir / **flipper** 22
soħen kartisim / **ticket agent** 17
sportay / **athlete** 15
sroħ na'al / **shoelace** 7
stav / **Fall** 5
sufat sheleg / **snowstorm** 5
sukar / **sugar** 10
sulam / **ladder** 23
sulam ħavalim / **rope ladder** 21
sulamot / **jungle gym** 8
sus / **horse** 9
sus nadneda / **rocking horse** 4
suson yam / **sea horse** 22
sveder / **sweater** 7
syaħ / **colt** 9

ta do'ar / **post-office box** 13
ta hakpa'a / **freezer** 3
ta mit'an / **trunk** 14
ta mit'an / **luggage compartment** 17
ta neħita / **landing capsule** 23
ta telefon / **phone booth** 13
ta'ar / **razor** 12
taba'at / **ring** 7
taba'ot / **rings** 23
tabaħ / **cook** 15
taf'ura / **scenery** 19
tafrit / **menu** 10
taħanat ħalal / **space station** 23
taħanat kaba'im / **fire station** 8
taħanat mishtara / **police station** 8
taħanat otobus / **bus stop** 16
taħanat rakevet / **train station** 8
taħshit / **jewel** 22
taħshitan / **jeweler** 15
taħtit / **saucer** 10
taħton / **bottom** 26
taklit / **record** 2
taklitan / **disc jockey** 15
taklitor / **compact disc** 2
talé / **lamb** 9
talmid / **student (male)** 1
talmida / **student (female)** 1
tamrur atzor / **stop sign** 16
tanin / **alligator** 20
tanur afiya / **oven** 3
tanur mikrogal / **microwave oven** 3
tapu'aħ / **apple** 6
tapu'aħ mesukar / **caramel apple** 21
tapuħey adama / **potatoes** 6
tapuz / **orange** 6
tarnegol / **rooster** 9
tarnegolet / **hen** 9
tarsis se'ar / **hair spray** 12
tasrit / **script** 19

tatzlum / **photograph** 4
tatzlum rentgen / **x ray** 11
tavas / **peacock** 20
tayas / **pilot** 17
ta'yeset mishné / **copilot** 17
ta'yish / **goat** 9
té / **tea** 10
te'ala / **channel** 32
te'ala / **canal** 32
teħnay televizya / **television repairer** 15
teker / **flat tire** 14
telefon / **telephone** 2
televizya / **television** 2
tenis / **tennis** 18
tenis shulħan / **table tennis** 18
tered / **spinach** 6
tesha / **nine** 31
teyvat do'ar / **mailbox** 13
teyvat negina / **music box** 4
teyvat otzar / **treasure chest** 22
tfarim / **claws** 20
tik gav / **backpack** 7
tik menahalim / **briefcase** 17
tik yad / **purse** 17
tikra / **ceiling** 2
tilboshet / **costume** 19
tinok / **baby** 9
tipat geshem / **raindrop** 5
tira / **castle** 25
tiras / **corn** 24
tish'im / **ninety** 31
tish'im ushmoné / **ninety-eight** 31
tish'im ushta'yim / **ninety-two** 31
tish'im va shesh / **ninety-six** 31
tish'im va sheva / **ninety-seven** 31
tish'im va tesha / **ninety-nine** 31
tish'im ve'aħat / **ninety-one** 31
tish'im ve'arba / **ninety-four** 31
tish'im ve'ħamesh / **ninety-five** 31
tish'im ve'shalosh / **ninety-three** 31
tisporet ktzutza / **crew cut** 12
tizmoret / **orchestra** 19
tizmoret / **band** 21
tlat ofan / **tricycle** 14
tmanun / **octopus** 22
tmuna / **picture** 1
tof / **drum** 19
toksido / **tuxedo** 4
tola'at / **worm** 5
tost / **toast** 10
totaħ / **cannon** 22
tov / **good** 26
traktor / **tractor** 9
trapez / **trapeze** 21
trigon kotzani / **stingray** 22
tris rafafot / **venetian blinds** 2
trombon / **trombone** 19
trufa / **medicine** 11
tsha esré / **nineteen** 31
tshi'i / **ninth** 31
tuba / **tuba** 19
tuki / **parrot** 20
tundra / **tundra** 32
turban / **turban** 21
tutim / **strawberries** 6
tvi'at regel / **footprint** 23
tza'atzu'im / **toys** 4
tza'if / **scarf** 7
tza'yad / **hunter** 24
tzaba / **painter** 15
tzafon / **north** 32
tzahov / **yellow** 28
tzalaħat / **plate** 10
tzalaħat / **hubcap** 14
tzalam / **photographer** 15
tzama / **braid** 12
tzamid / **bracelet** 7
tzar / **narrow** 26
tzav / **turtle** 20
tzav yam / **sea turtle** 22
tzavaron / **collar** 7
tzel / **shadow** 9
tzemaħ / **plant** 1
tzemer gefen matok / **cotton candy** 21
tzeva / **crayon** 1
tzeva / **paint** 24, 1
tzfardé'a / **frog** 9
tzfon amerika / **North America** 32
tzfon ma'arav / **northwest** 32
tzfon mizraħ / **northeast** 32
tzi'yur me'arot / **cave drawing** 24
tzidpa / **clam** 22
tzilinder / **top hat** 4
tzinok / **dungeon** 25
tzinor avir / **air hose** 14
tzinor hashkaya / **garden hose** 5
tzipor / **bird** 5
tziporen / **toenail** 12
tziporen / **fingernail** 12
tzmig / **tire** 14
tzniħa ħofshit / **skydiving** 18
tzohar / **porthole** 22
tzolelan / **scuba diver** 22
tzolelet / **submarine** 22
tzomet / **intersection** 16
tzvi / **deer** 20

uga / **cake** 10
ugiyot / **cookies** 6
ukaf / **saddle** 25
ulam / **auditorium** 19
umtza / **steak** 10
urva / **stable** 25

varod / **pink** 28

English-Hebrew Glossary and Index

above	26	מֵעַל
accordion	19	אַקּוֹרְדְּיוֹן
acrobat	21	לוּלְיָן
actor	19	שַׂחְקָן
actress	19	שַׂחְקָנִית
address	13	כְּתֹבֶת
Africa	32	אַפְרִיקָה
air hose	14	צִינּוֹר אֲוִויר
air-traffic controller	17	פַּקַּחִית טִיסָה
airplane	17, 16	מָטוֹס
alarm clock	2	שְׁעוֹן מְעוֹרֵר
alien	23	יְצוּר מֵעוֹלָם אַחֵר
alligator	20	תַּנִּין
alphabet	1	אָלֶף בֵּית
ambulance	16	אַמְבּוּלַנְס
anchor	22	עוֹגֶן
angelfish	22	דַּג מַלְאָךְ
animals	20	בַּעֲלֵי-חַיִּים
ankle	11	קַרְסוֹל
ant	9	נְמָלָה
Antarctica	32	אַנְטַרְקְטִיקָה
antenna	23	אַנְטֶנָּה
anvil	25	סַדָּן
apartment building	8	בֵּית דִּירוֹת
apple	6	תַּפּוּחַ
apron	3	סִינּוֹר
aquarium	1	אַקְוַורְיוּם
archer	25	קַשָּׁת
architect	15	אַדְרִיכָלִית
Arctic Ocean	32	הָאוֹקְיָינוֹס הָאַרְקְטִי
arithmetic problem	1	בְּעָיָה בְּחֶשְׁבּוֹן
arm	11	זְרוֹעַ
armchair	2	כּוּרְסָה
armor	25	שִׁרְיוֹן
arrow	25	חֵץ
arrowhead	24	רֹאשׁ חֵץ
artist	15	אָמָּן
Asia	32	אַסְיָה
asteroid	23	אַסְטְרוֹאִיד
astronaut	23	אִישׁ חָלָל
astronomer	15	אַסְטְרוֹנוֹם
athlete	15	סְפּוֹרְטַאי
Atlantic Ocean	32	הָאוֹקְיָינוֹס הָאַטְלַנְטִי
audience	19	קָהָל
auditorium	19	אוּלָם
aunt	29	דּוֹדָה
Australia	32	אוֹסְטְרַלְיָה
automatic teller	13	כַּסְפּוֹמָט
avocado	6	אֲבוֹקָדוֹ
ax	25	גַּרְזֶן
baby	9	תִּינוֹק
baby carriage	16	עֲגָלַת תִּינוֹק
back	11	גַּב
backpack	7	תִּיק גַּב
backseat	14	מוֹשָׁב אֲחוֹרִי
bad	26	רַע
badminton	18	כַּדּוּר נוֹצִית
baggage cart	17	עֲגָלַת מִטְעָן
baggage check-in	17	קְלִיטַת מִטְעָן
baggage claim	17	מַסּוֹעַ מִטְעָן
baggage handler	17	סַבָּל
bakery	8	מַאֲפִיָּה
balcony	8	מִרְפֶּסֶת
bald	12	קֵירֵחַ
ball gown	4	שִׂמְלַת נֶשֶׁף
ballet slippers	19	נַעֲלֵי בַּלֶּט
balloon	21	בַּלּוֹן
banana	6	בָּנָנָה
band	21	תִּזְמוֹרֶת
bandage	11	פְּלַסְטֶר
bangs	12	פּוֹנִי
banker	15	בַּנְקָאִית
banner	25	דֶּגֶל
barbecue	5	אַסְכָּלָה
barber	12	סַפָּר
bareback rider	21	לַהֲטוּטָן רְכִיבָה
barn	9	אָסָם
barnacle	22	דַּג הַשַּׁבְּלוּל
barrette	12	מַכְבֵּנָה
baseball	18	כַּדּוּר בֵּייסְבּוֹל
baseball	18	בֵּייסְבּוֹל
basket	24	סַל
basketball	18	כַּדּוּרְסַל
bat	18	אַלָּה
bat	25	עֲטַלֵּף
bathing suit	7	בֶּגֶד יָם
bathrobe	7	חֲלוּק רַחְצָה
bathroom	2	חֲדַר אַמְבַּטְיָה
bathtub	2	אַמְבַּטְיָה
baton	21	שַׁרְבִיט
bay	32	מִפְרָץ
beach	8	חוֹף
beak	20	מַקּוֹר
beaker	23	כְּלִי מַעְבָּדָה
bear	20	דּוֹב
bear cub	20	דּוּבּוֹן
beard	12	זָקָן
bed	2	מִיטָּה
bedroom	2	חֲדַר שֵׁינָה
bees	9	דְּבוֹרִים
behind	26	מֵאָחוֹר
bell	1	פַּעֲמוֹן
belt	7	חֲגוֹרָה
bench	8	סַפְסָל
between	26	בֵּין
bicycle	18, 16, 14	אוֹפַנַּיִים
bicycle chain	14	שַׁרְשֶׁרֶת
big top	21	הָאוֹהֶל הַמֶּרְכָּזִי
bill	13	שְׁטָר
billion	31	מִילְיַארְד
binoculars	17	מִשְׁקֶפֶת
bird	5	צִיפּוֹר
bird's nest	5	קֵן שֶׁל צִיפּוֹר
birthday party	10	מְסִיבַּת יוֹם הוּלֶּדֶת
bison	24	בִּיזוֹן
black	28, 12	שָׁחוֹר
blacksmith	25	נַפָּח
blanket	2	שְׂמִיכָה
blimp	16	סְפִינַת אֲוִויר
blocks	4	קוּבִּיּוֹת
blond	12	בְּלוֹנְדִּינִי
blood	11	דָּם
blouse	7	כּוּתֹּנֶת
blow dryer	12	מְיַיבֵּשׁ שֵׂעָר
blue	28	כָּחוֹל
board	3	קֶרֶשׁ
boat	16	סְפִינָה
bone	24	עֶצֶם
book	1	סֵפֶר
bookcase	1	כּוֹנָנִית סְפָרִים
bookseller	15	מוֹכֵר סְפָרִים
bookstore	8	חֲנוּת סְפָרִים
boots	7	מַגָּפַיִים
bottle	6	בַּקְבּוּק
bottom	26	תַּחְתּוֹן
boulder	24	סֶלַע גָּדוֹל
bow	13	לוּלָאָה
bow	25, 19	קֶשֶׁת
bowl	10	קְעָרָה
bowling	18	כַּדּוֹרֶת
box	4	קוּפְסָה
boxing	18	אִגְרוּף
boxing gloves	18	כְּפָפוֹת אִגְרוּף
boy	9	יֶלֶד
bracelet	7	צָמִיד
braces	11	גֶּשֶׁר
braid	12	צַמָּה
brake lights	14	אוֹרוֹת עֲצִירָה
branch	5	עָנָף
bread	6	לֶחֶם
break	27	לִשְׁבּוֹר
breakfast	10	אֲרוּחַת בּוֹקֶר
brick	3	לְבֵנָה
bridge	16	גֶּשֶׁר
briefcase	17	תִּיק מְנַהֲלִים
broccoli	10	בְּרוֹקוֹלִי
broom	3	מַטְאֲטֵא
brother	29	אָח
brown	28, 12	חוּם
brush	12	מִבְרֶשֶׁת
bubble	22	בּוּעָה
bucket	24	דְּלִי
buckle	7	אַבְזָם
building	8	בִּנְיָין
bull	9	פַּר
bulletin board	1	לוּחַ מוֹדָעוֹת
bun	12	פְּקַעַת
buoy	22	מָצוֹף
bus	16	אוֹטוֹבּוּס
bus driver	15	נַהֶגֶת אוֹטוֹבּוּס
bus stop	16	תַּחֲנַת אוֹטוֹבּוּס
bush	5	שִׂיחַ
butcher	15	קַצָּב
butcher shop	8	אִטְלִיז
butter	6	חֶמְאָה
butterfly	5	פַּרְפַּר
button	7	כַּפְתּוֹר
buy	27	לִקְנוֹת
cabbage	6	כְּרוּב
cactus	1	קַקְטוּס
cage	21	כְּלוּב

cake 10 עוּגָה
calculator 1 מַחְשְׁבוֹן
calendar 1 לוּחַ שָׁנָה
calf 9 עֵגֶל
camel 20 גָּמָל
camera 21, 17 מַצְלֵמָה
camper 16 קְרָוָן
can 6 פַּחִית
canal 32 תְּעָלָה
candle 10 נֵר
candy 6 מַמְתַּקִּים
cane 11 מַקֵּל
cannon 22 תּוֹתָח
canoe 16 קָנוּ
cap 7 כּוֹבַע צֶמֶר
cape 21 גְּלִימָה
cape 32 כֵּף
car 16 מְכוֹנִית
car racing 18 מֵירוֹץ מְכוֹנִיּוֹת
car wash 14 שְׁטִיפַת מְכוֹנִיּוֹת
caramel apple 21 תַּפּוּחַ מְסוּכָּר
cardinal numbers 31 מִסְפָּרִים יְסוֹדִיִּים
cards 4 קְלָפִים
cargo bay 23 שֶׁטַח מִטְעָן
carpenter 15 נַגָּר
carpet 2 שָׁטִיחַ
carrots 6 גֶּזֶר
carry 27 לִסְחוֹב
cart 24 עֲגָלָה
cartwheel 21 גַּלְגִּילוֹן
cash register 6 קוּפָּה רוֹשֶׁמֶת
cashier 6 קוּפָּאִית
cassette player 2 רְשַׁמְקוֹל
cassette tape 2 קַלֶּטֶת
cast 11 גֶּבֶס
castle 25 טִירָה
cat 9 חָתוּל
catch 27 לִתְפּוֹס
cave 24 מְעָרָה
cave drawing 24 צִיּוּר מְעָרוֹת
cave dwellers 24 שׁוֹכְנֵי מְעָרוֹת
ceiling 2 תִּקְרָה
celery 10 סֶלֶרִי
cello 19 צֶ'לוֹ
cellophane tape 1 נְיָר דֶּבֶק
cement mixer 16 מְעַרְבֵּל בֶּטוֹן
cereal 6 דְּגָנִים
chain mail 25 שִׁרְיוֹן קַשְׂקַשִּׂים
chair 3 כִּסֵּא
chalk 1 גִּיר
chalkboard 1 לוּחַ
(chalkboard) eraser 1 סְפוֹג מְחִיקָה
channel 32 תְּעָלָה
check 13 הַמְחָאָה
checkbook 13 פִּנְקַס הַמְחָאוֹת
checkers 4 דַּמְקָה
cheek 11 לֶחִי
cheese 6 גְּבִינָה
cherries 6 דּוּבְדְּבָנִים
chess 4 שַׁחְמָט
chest 11 חָזֶה
chick 9 אֶפְרוֹחַ
chicken 10 עוֹף

children 19 יְלָדִים
chimney 2 אֲרוּבָּה
chin 11 סַנְטֵר
chocolate 6 שׁוֹקוֹלָד
church 8 כְּנֵסִיָּה
circle 30 מַעְגָּל
circus parade 21 מִצְעַד הַקִּרְקָס
clam 22 צִדְפָּה
clarinet 19 קְלַרְינֶט
claws 20 טְפָרִים
clay 24 חוֹמֶר
clean 26 נָקִי
climb 27 לְטַפֵּס
clock 1 שָׁעוֹן
close 27 לִסְגּוֹר
closed 26 סָגוּר
closet 2 אֲרוֹן בְּגָדִים
cloth 24 אָרִיג
clothes dryer 3 מְיַבֵּשׁ כְּבִיסָה
clothing store 8 חֲנוּת בְּגָדִים
clouds 5 עֲנָנִים
clown 21 לֵיצָן
club 24 אַלָּה
coat 7 מְעִיל
cobweb 4 קוּרֵי עַכָּבִישׁ
coffee 10 קָפֶה
coin 13 מַטְבֵּעַ
cold 26 קַר
collar 7 צַוָּארוֹן
colored pencils 1 עֶפְרוֹנוֹת צִבְעוֹנִיִּים
coloring book 4 חוֹבֶרֶת צְבִיעָה
colt 9 סְיָח
comb 12 מַסְרֵק
come 27 לָבוֹא
comet 23 כּוֹכַב שָׁבִיט
comic books 4 חוֹבְרוֹת מְצוּיָּרוֹת
compact disc 2 תַּקְלִיטוֹר
compass 1 מְחוּגָה
compass 32 מַצְפֵּן
computer 23 מַחְשֵׁב
computer programmer 15 מְתַכְנֶתֶת מַחְשְׁבִים
concorde 17 קוֹנְקוֹרְד
conductor 19 מְנַצֵּחַ
cone 30 חָרוּט
constellation 23 מַעֲרֶכֶת כּוֹכָבִים
construction worker 15 בַּנַּאי
control panel 23 לוּחַ בַּקָּרָה
control tower 17 מִגְדַּל פִּיקּוּחַ
cook 15 טַבָּח
cook 27 לְבַשֵּׁל
cookies 6 עוּגִיּוֹת
copilot 17 טַיֶּסֶת מִשְׁנֶה
coral 22 אַלְמוֹג
coral reef 22 רִיף אַלְמוּגִּים
corn 24 תִּירָס
corner 8 פִּינָּה
costume 19 תִּלְבּוֹשֶׁת
cotton candy 21 צֶמֶר גֶּפֶן מָתוֹק
counter 3 דֶּלְפֵּק
court jester 25 לֵיצַן חָצֵר
courtyard 25 חָצֵר
cousin 29 בֶּן-דּוֹד

cousin 29 בַּת-דּוֹדָה
coveralls 14 סַרְבָּל
cow 9 פָּרָה
cowboy 15 בּוֹקֵר
cowboy boots 4 מַגָּפֵי בּוֹקְרִים
cowboy hat 4 כּוֹבַע בּוֹקְרִים
crab 22 סַרְטָן
crackers 6 קְרֶקֶרִים
cradle 4 עֲרִיסָה
crane 8 עֲגוּרָן
crater 23 מַכְתֵּשׁ
crayon 1 צֶבַע
cream 10 שַׁמֶּנֶת
credit card 13 כַּרְטִיס אַשְׁרַאי
crew cut 12 תִּסְפּוֹרֶת קְצוּצָה
crop 24 יְבוּל
cross-country skiing 18 קְרוֹס קַנְטְרִי סְקִיאִינְג
crosswalk 16 מַעֲבַר חֲצִיָּה
crown 25 כֶּתֶר
cruise ship 16 אֳנִיַּית נוֹסְעִים
crutch 11 קַב
cry 27 לִבְכּוֹת
cube 30 קוּבִּיָּה
cup 10 סֵפֶל
curlers 12 רוֹלִים
curling iron 12 מְתַלְתֵּל
curly 12 מְתוּלְתָּל
curtain 19 מָסָךְ
curtains 2 וִילוֹן
customs officer 17 מוֹכֶסֶת
cut 27 לִגְזוֹר
cycling 18 רְכִיבָה עַל אוֹפַנַּיִם
cylinder 30 גָּלִיל
cymbals 19 מְצִלְתַּיִם

dance 27 לִרְקוֹד
dancer 19 רַקְדָנִית
dark 26 כֵּהֶה
dashboard 14 לוּחַ שְׁעוֹנִים
daughter 29 בַּת
deck 5 מִרְפֶּסֶת
deer 20 צְבִי
dental floss 11 חוּט דֶּנְטָלִי
dental hygienist 11 שִׁינָּנִית
dentist 11 רוֹפֵא שִׁינַּיִם
desert 32 מִדְבָּר
dice 4 קוּבִּיּוֹת
difficult 26 קָשֶׁה
dig 27 לַחְפּוֹר
dining room 2 חֲדַר אוֹכֶל
dinner 10 אֲרוּחַת עֶרֶב
dinosaur 24 דִּינוֹזָאוּר
dirt 9 עָפָר
dirty 26 מְלוּכְלָךְ
disc jockey 15 תַּקְלִיטָן
dishes 3 כֵּלִים
dishwasher 3 מְדִיחַ כֵּלִים
dive 27 לִקְפּוֹץ לַמַּיִם
diving 18 קְפִיצָה לַמַּיִם
dock 16 מֵזַח
doctor 11 רוֹפְאָה
dog 9 כֶּלֶב

garage	14	מוּסָךְ
garden hose	5	צִינּוֹר הַשְׁקָיָה
gardener	15	גַּנָּן
garment bag	17	מִנְשָׂא בְּגָדִים
gas cap	14	מִכְסֶה דֶּלֶק
gas pump	14	מַשְׁאֵבַת דֶּלֶק
gate	17	שַׁעַר
giant	25	עֲנָק
gift	10	מַתָּנָה
gills	22	זִימִים
giraffe	20	ג׳ִירָפָה
girl	9	יַלְדָּה
give	27	לָתֵת
glacier	32	קַרְחוֹן
glass	10	כּוֹס
glasses	7	מִשְׁקָפַיִים
globe	1	גְּלוֹבּוּס
gloves	7	כְּפָפוֹת
glue	1	דֶּבֶק
go	27	לָלֶכֶת
go!	16	סַע!
goat	9	תַּיִשׁ
goggles	18	מִשְׁקְפֵי שְׂחִיָּיה
gold	28, 22	זָהָב
golf	18	גּוֹלְף
golf club	18	אַלַּת גּוֹלְף
good	26	טוֹב
goose	9	אַוָּז
gorilla	20	גּוֹרִילָה
gosling	9	אַוָּזוֹן
grandfather ,grandpa	29	סַבָּא
grandmother ,grandma	29	סַבְתָּא
grapefruit	6	אֶשְׁכּוֹלִית
grapes	6	עֲנָבִים
grass	9	דֶּשֶׁא
grasshopper	5	חָגָב
gray	28	אָפוֹר
green	28	יָרוֹק
green beans	6	שְׁעוּעִית יְרוּקָּה
grocery story	8	חֲנוּת מַכּוֹלֶת
guitar	19	גִּיטָרָה
gulf	32	מִפְרָץ
gym shoes	7	נַעֲלֵי הִתְעַמְּלוּת
gymnastics	18	הִתְעַמְּלוּת
hair	12	שֵׂעָר
hair dryer	12	מְיַיבֵּשׁ שֵׂעָר
hair spray	12	תַּרְסִיס שֵׂעָר
hairstylist	12	מְעַצֶּבֶת שֵׂעָר
half	31	חֲצִי
ham	10	נַקְנִיק חֲזִיר
hamburger	10	הַמְבּוּרְגֶר
hammer	3	פַּטִּישׁ
hammock	5	עַרְסָל
hand	1	מָחוֹג
hand	11	יָד
hand brake	14	מַעְצוֹר יָד
handkerchief	7	מִטְפַּחַת
handlebars	14	כִּידוֹן
handstand	21	עֲמִידַת יָדַיִים
hang glider	16	גִּלְשָׁן אֲוִויר
hangar	17	סְכָכַת מְטוֹסִים
hanger	2	קוֹלָב
happy	26	שָׂמֵחַ
hard	26	קָשֶׁה
harp	19	נֵבֶל
hat	7, 4	כּוֹבַע
hay	9	שַׁחַת
head	11	רֹאשׁ
headlight	14	אוֹר קִדְמִי
headset	17	אוֹזְנִיּוֹת
headstand	21	עֲמִידַת רֹאשׁ
heavy	26	כָּבֵד
helicopter	16	מַסּוֹק
helm	22	הֶגֶה
helmet	18	קַסְדָּה
hen	9	תַּרְנְגוֹלֶת
high jump	18	קְפִיצָה לַגּוֹבַהּ
hiking boots	7	נַעֲלֵי הֲלִיכָה
hill	9	גִּבְעָה
hippopotamus	20	הִיפּוֹפּוֹטָם
hockey	18	הוֹקִי
hole punch	1	מְחוֹרֵר
hood	7	בַּרְדָּס
hood	14	מִכְסֵה הַמָּנוֹעַ
hoof	20	פַּרְסָה
hoop	21	חִישּׁוּק
horns	20, 9	קַרְנַיִים
horse	9	סוּס
horse racing	18	מֵירוֹץ סוּסִים
horseback riding	18	רְכִיבָה עַל סוּסִים
horseshoe	25	פַּרְסָה
hospital	8	בֵּית-חוֹלִים
hot	26	חַם
hot-air balloon	16	כַּדּוּר פּוֹרֵחַ
hotel	8	בֵּית מָלוֹן
hubcap	14	צַלַּחַת
hump	20	דַּבֶּשֶׁת
hundred	31	מֵאָה
hundred thousand	31	מֵאָה אֶלֶף
hunter	24	צַיָּיד
hurdles	18	מְשׂוּכוֹת
hut	24	בִּקְתָּה
hypodermic needle	11	מַזְרֵק
ice	5	קֶרַח
ice cream	10	גְּלִידָה
ice cubes	3	קוּבִּיּוֹת קֶרַח
iceberg	32	קַרְחוֹן
icecap	32	כִּיפַּת קֶרַח
icicle	5	נְטִיף קֶרַח
in front of	26	לִפְנֵי
Indian Ocean	32	הָאוֹקְיָינוֹס הַהוֹדִי
ink pad	13	כָּרִית דְּיוֹ
insect	24	חֶרֶק
inside	26	בִּפְנִים
intersection	16	צוֹמֶת
iron	3	מַגְהֵץ
ironing board	3	לוּחַ גִּיהוּץ
island	32	אִי
jack	14	מַגְבֵּהַּ
jacket	7	ז׳ָקֶט
jaguar	20	יָגוּאָר
jail	8	בֵּית כֶּלֶא
jam	10	רִיבָּה
jeans	7	ג׳ִינְס
jeep	16	ג׳ִיפּ
jellyfish	22	מְדוּזָה
jewel	22	תַּכְשִׁיט
jeweler	15	תַּכְשִׁיטָן
jigsaw puzzle	4	פָּאזֶל
jogging	18	ג׳וֹגִינְג
judge	15	שׁוֹפֶטֶת
juggle	27	לְלַהֲטֵט
juggler	21	לַהֲטוּטָן
jump	27	לִקְפּוֹץ
jump rope	4	דַּלְגִּית
jungle	32	ג׳וּנְגֶל
jungle gym	8	סוּלָּמוֹת
kangaroo	20	קֶנְגּוּרוּ
ketchup	10	קֶטְשׁוֹפּ
kettle	3	קוּמְקוּם
key	13	מַפְתֵּחַ
kick	27	לִבְעוֹט
kickstand	14	רַגְלִית
kid	9	גְּדִי
kiln	24	כִּבְשָׁן
king	25	מֶלֶךְ
kitchen	2	מִטְבָּח
kite	5	עֲפִיפוֹן
kitten	9	חֲתַלְתּוּל
knee	11	בֶּרֶךְ
knife	10	סַכִּין
knight	25	אַבִּיר
knitting needles	4	מַסְרֵגוֹת
knot	13	קֶשֶׁר
lab coat	23	חֲלוּק מַעְבָּדָה
label	13	פִּתְקִית
laboratory	23	מַעְבָּדָה
ladder	23	סוּלָּם
lake	32	אֲגַם
lamb	9	טָלֶה
lamp	2	מְנוֹרָה
lance	25	רוֹמַח
landing capsule	23	תָּא נְחִיתָה
landing gear	17	כַּן נְחִיתָה
large	26	גָּדוֹל
laugh	27	לִצְחוֹק
laundry	3	כְּבִיסָה
laundry detergent	3	אַבְקַת כְּבִיסָה
lawn mower	5	מַכְסֵחַת דֶּשֶׁא
lawyer	15	עוֹרֶכֶת דִּין
leaf	5	עָלֶה
leather	24	עוֹר
left	26	שְׂמֹאל
leg	11	רֶגֶל
lemon	6	לִימוֹן
leopard	20	בַּרְדְּלָס
leotard	19	בֶּגֶד גּוּף
letter	13	מִכְתָּב
letter carrier	15	דַּוָּור
lettuce	6	חַסָּה
librarian	15	סַפְרָן
light	26	בָּהִיר
light	26	קַל
light bulb	21, 4	נוּרָה

lighthouse	16	מִגְדַּלּוֹר
lightning	5	בָּרָק
lime	6	לַיִים
lion	21, 20	אַרְיֵה
lion tamer	21	מְאַלֵּף אֲרָיוֹת
lips	11	שְׂפָתַיִים
lipstick	12	שְׂפָתוֹן
listen (to)	27	לְהַקְשִׁיב
living room	2	חֲדַר מְגוּרִים
lizard	20	לְטָאָה
lobster	22	סַרְטָן
lock	13	מַנְעוּל
log	5	בּוּל עֵץ
long	26, 12	אָרוֹךְ
long jump	18	קְפִיצָה לְרוֹחַק
look for	27	לְחַפֵּשׂ
loom	24	נוֹל
loudspeaker	1	רַמְקוֹל
luggage compartment	17	תָּא מִטְעָן
lunar rover	23	רֶכֶב חָלָל
lunch	10	אֲרוּחַת צָהֳרַיִים
magazines	11	כִּתְבֵי עֵת
magic wand	25	מַטֵּה קְסָמִים
magician	21	קוֹסֵם
magnet	4	מַגְנֵט
mail slot	13	חָרִיץ
mailbag	13	שַׂק דּוֹאַר
mailbox	13	תֵּיבַת דּוֹאַר
makeup	19	אִיפּוּר
mammoth	24	מָמוּתָה
man	9	גֶּבֶר
mane	20	רַעְמָה
manhole cover	8	מִכְסֵה תְּעָלַת בִּיּוּב
manicurist	12	מָנִיקוּרִיסְטִית
map	1	מַפָּה
marbles	4	גּוּלוֹת
mascara	12	מַסְקָרָה
mask	19	מַסֵּכָה
mask	22	מַסֵּכַת צְלִילָה
master of ceremonies	19	מַנְחֶה
matches	5	גַּפְרוּרִים
meals	10	אֲרוּחוֹת
meat	6	בָּשָׂר
mechanic	14	מְכוֹנַאי
medal	18	מֶדַלְיָה
medicine	11	תְּרוּפָה
medicine cabinet	2	אֲרוֹן תְּרוּפוֹת
medium	26	בֵּינוֹנִי
melon	6	מֶלוֹן
menu	10	תַּפְרִיט
metal detector	17	גַּלַּאי מַתָּכוֹת
meteor shower	23	מְטַר מֶטֶאוֹרִים
microphone	19	מִיקְרוֹפוֹן
microscope	23	מִיקְרוֹסְקוֹפּ
microwave oven	3	תַּנּוּר מִיקְרוֹגַל
milk	6	חָלָב
million	31	מִילְיוֹן
minstrel	25	זַמָּר נוֹדֵד
mirror	2	מַרְאָה
mittens	7	כְּפָפוֹת
moat	25	חֲפִיר מָגֵן
model	15	דּוּגְמָנִית
money	6	כֶּסֶף
monkey	20	קוֹף
moon	23	יָרֵחַ
moon rock	23	סֶלַע יָרֵחַ
mop	3	סְחָבָה עַל מַקֵּל
mother ,mom	29	אִימָּא
motorboat	16	סִירַת מָנוֹעַ
motorcycle	16	אוֹפַנּוֹעַ
mountains	32	הָרִים
mouse	9	עַכְבָּר
mousse	12	מוּס
mouth	11	פֶּה
movie projector	4	מַקְרֵנָה
movie theater	8	בֵּית-קוֹלְנוֹעַ
mud	5	בּוֹץ
museum	8	מוּזֵיאוֹן
mushroom	10	פִּטְרִיָּה
music box	4	תֵּיבַת נְגִינָה
mustache	12	שָׂפָם
mustard	10	חַרְדָּל
nail	3	מַסְמֵר
nail clippers	12	קוֹצֵץ צִיפּוֹרְנַיִים
nail file	12	פְּצִירָה
nail polish	12	לַק
napkin	10	מַפִּית
narrow	26	צַר
navigator	17	נַוָּט
near	26	קָרוֹב
nebula	23	עַרְפִילִית
necklace	7	שַׁרְשֶׁרֶת
net	18	רֶשֶׁת
new	26	חָדָשׁ
newspaper	8	עִיתּוֹן
next to	26	לְיַד
night	21	לַיְלָה
night table	2	שׁוּלְחַן לַיְלָה
nine	31	תֵּשַׁע
nineteen	31	תְּשַׁע-עֶשְׂרֵה
ninety	31	תִּשְׁעִים
ninety-eight	31	תִּשְׁעִים וּשְׁמוֹנֶה
ninety-five	31	תִּשְׁעִים וְחָמֵשׁ
ninety-four	31	תִּשְׁעִים וְאַרְבַּע
ninety-nine	31	תִּשְׁעִים וְתֵשַׁע
ninety-one	31	תִּשְׁעִים וְאַחַת
ninety-seven	31	תִּשְׁעִים וָשֶׁבַע
ninety-six	31	תִּשְׁעִים וָשֵׁשׁ
ninety-three	31	תִּשְׁעִים וְשָׁלוֹשׁ
ninety-two	31	תִּשְׁעִים וּשְׁתַּיִים
ninth	31	תְּשִׁיעִי
noodles	10	אִטְרִיּוֹת
north	32	צָפוֹן
North America	32	צְפוֹן אֲמֶרִיקָה
North Pole	32	הַקּוֹטֶב הַצְּפוֹנִי
northeast	32	צְפוֹן מִזְרָח
northwest	32	צְפוֹן מַעֲרָב
nose	11	אַף
notebook	1	מַחְבֶּרֶת
notepad	13	דַּפְדֶּפֶת
numbers	1	מִסְפָּרִים
nurse	11	אָח
nuts	6	אֱגוֹזִים
oar	16	מָשׁוֹט
oasis	32	נְוֵה מִדְבָּר
octagon	30	מְתוּמָּן
octopus	22	תְּמָנוּן
off	26	מְכוּבֶּה
oil	14	שֶׁמֶן
old	26	יָשָׁן
omelet	10	חֲבִיתָה
on	26	דּוֹלֵק
on top of	26	עַל
one	31	אַחַת
onions	6	בָּצָל
open	26	פָּתוּחַ
open	27	לִפְתּוֹחַ
optician	15	אוֹפְּטִיקָאִית
orange	6	תַּפּוּז
orange	28	כָּתוֹם
orchestra	19	תִּזְמוֹרֶת
orchestra pit	19	מוֹשַׁב הַתִּזְמוֹרֶת
ordinal numbers	31	מִסְפָּרִים סִידּוּרִיִּים
ostrich	20	יָעֵן
outside	26	בַּחוּץ
oval	30	אֶלִּיפְּסָה
oven	3	תַּנּוּר אֲפִיָּה
owl	20	יַנְשׁוּף
oxygen tank	22	מְכַל חַמְצָן
Pacific Ocean	32	הָאוֹקְיָינוֹס הַשָּׁקֵט
package	13	חֲבִילָה
packing tape	13	נְיַיר דֶּבֶק
paint	24, 1	צֶבַע
paint	27	לְצַיֵּיר
paintbrush	1	מִכְחוֹל
painter	15	צַבָּע
pajamas	7	פִּיגָ'מָה
pan	3	מַחֲבַת
panda	20	פַּנְדָּה
pants	7	מִכְנָסַיִים
paper	1	נְיָיר
paper clip	13	מְהַדֵּק
paper towels	3	מַגָּבוֹת נְיָיר
parachute	18	מַצְנֵחַ
paramedic	15	חוֹבֵשׁ
park	8	גַּן
parking lot	8	חֲנָיוֹן
parking meter	8	מַדְחָן
parrot	20	תּוּכִּי
part	12	שְׁבִיל
passenger	17	נוֹסֵעַ
passenger's seat	14	מוֹשָׁב קִדְמִי
passport	17	דַּרְכּוֹן
patient	11	מְטוּפָּל
paw	20	כַּף
peach	6	אֲפַרְסֵק
peacock	20	טַוָּוס
peanuts	21	בּוֹטְנִים
peas	6	אֲפוּנָה
pedal	14	דַּוְושָׁה
pedicurist	12	פֶּדִיקוּרִיסְטִית
pen	1	עֵט
pencil	1	עִיפָּרוֹן
pencil sharpener	1	מְחַדֵּד
(pencil) eraser	1	מוֹחֵק

penguin	20	פִּינְגְּוִוין
peninsula	32	חֲצִי אִי
pepper	10	פִּלְפֵּל
petal	5	עֲלֵה כּוֹתֶרֶת
pharmacist	15	רוֹקַחַת
phone booth	13	תָּא טֶלֶפוֹן
photo album	4	אַלְבּוֹם תְּמוּנוֹת
photograph	4	תַּצְלוּם
photographer	15	צַלָּם
piano	19	פְּסַנְתֵּר
picnic	9	פִּיקְנִיק
picture	1	תְּמוּנָה
picture frame	4	מִסְגֶּרֶת
pie	6	פַּאי
pig	9	חֲזִיר
piggy bank	13	קוּפַּת חִיסָּכוֹן
piglet	9	חֲזִירוֹן
pill	11	כַּדּוּר
pillow	2	כַּר
pilot	17	טַיָּס
pineapple	6	אֲנָנָס
pink	28	וָרוֹד
plain	32	מִישׁוֹר
planet	23	כּוֹכַב לֶכֶת
plant	1	צֶמַח
plate	10	צַלַּחַת
play (a game)	27	לְשַׂחֵק
play (an instrument)	27	לְנַגֵּן
playground	8	גַּן מִשְׂחָקִים
pliers	14	פְּלַיֶּר
plumber	15	שְׁרַבְרַב
pocket	7	כִּיס
point (at)	27	לְהַצְבִּיעַ
polar bear	20	דּוֹב קוֹטֶב
police car	16	נַיֶּידֶת מִשְׁטָרָה
police station	8	תַּחֲנַת מִשְׁטָרָה
policeman	15	שׁוֹטֵר
policewoman	15	שׁוֹטֶרֶת
pond	9	בְּרֵכָה
ponytail	12	קוּקוּ
popcorn	21	פּוֹפְּקוֹרְן
porter	17	סַבָּל
porthole	22	צוֹהַר
post-office box	13	תָּא דּוֹאַר
postal worker	13	דַּוָּור
postcard	13	גְּלוּיָה
poster	2	פּוֹסְטֶר
postmark	13	חוֹתֶמֶת דּוֹאַר
pot	24	כְּלִי
potato chips	6	צִ'יפְּס
potatoes	6	תַּפּוּחֵי-אֲדָמָה
potter	24	קַדָּר
pour	27	לִשְׁפּוֹךְ
powder	12	פּוּדְרָה
price	6	מְחִיר
prince	25	נָסִיךְ
princess	25	נְסִיכָה
propeller	17	מַדְחֵף
protractor	1	מַד זָווִית
pterodactyl	24	לְטָאָה מְעוֹפֶפֶת
puddle	5	שְׁלוּלִית
pull	27	לִמְשׁוֹךְ
pupil desk	1	שׁוּלְחַן הַתַּלְמִיד
puppet	4	בּוּבָּה
puppy	9	כְּלַבְלָב
purple	28	סָגוֹל
purse	17	תִּיק יָד
push	27	לִדְחוֹף
queen	25	מַלְכָּה
quiver	25	אַשְׁפַּת חִצִּים
rabbit	9	אַרְנָב
race car	14	מְכוֹנִית מֵירוֹץ
racket	18	מַחְבֵּט
radar screen	17	מָסַךְ מַכָּ"ם
radio	2	רַדְיוֹ
rag	14	סְמַרְטוּט
rain	5	גֶּשֶׁם
rainbow	5	קֶשֶׁת
raincoat	7	מְעִיל גֶּשֶׁם
raindrop	5	טִיפַּת גֶּשֶׁם
rake	5	מַגְרֵפָה
raspberries	6	פֶּטֶל
rat	25	חוּלְדָּה
razor	12	תַּעַר
read	27	לִקְרוֹא
rearview mirror	14	מַרְאָה אֲחוֹרִית
receive	27	לְקַבֵּל
receptionist	13	פְּקִידַת קַבָּלָה
record	2	תַּקְלִיט
record player	2	פָּטֵיפוֹן
rectangle	30	מַלְבֵּן
red	12	ג'ִינְג'ִי
red	28	אָדוֹם
referee	18	שׁוֹפֵט
reflectors	14	מַחֲזִיר אוֹר
refrigerator	3	מְקָרֵר
reins	25	רֶסֶן
reporter	15	כַּתָּב
rest rooms	21	שֵׁירוּתִים
restaurant	8	מִסְעָדָה
return address	13	כְּתוֹבֶת הַשּׁוֹלֵחַ
rhinoceros	20	קַרְנַף
rice	10	אוֹרֶז
ride a bicycle	27	לִרְכּוֹב עַל אוֹפַנַּיִים
right	26	יָמִין
ring	7	טַבַּעַת
ring	21	זִירָה
ringmaster	21	מַנְחֶה
rings	23	טַבָּעוֹת
river	32	נָהָר
road	9	דֶּרֶךְ
roar	27	לִשְׁאוֹג
robot	23	רוֹבּוֹט
rock	24	סֶלַע
rocket	23	רָקֵטָה
rocking chair	4, 2	כִּיסֵּא נַדְנֵדָה
rocking horse	4	סוּס נַדְנֵדָה
roller skates	16	גַּלְגִּלִּיּוֹת
roof	2	גַּג
rooster	9	תַּרְנְגוֹל
rope	21, 19	חֶבֶל
rope ladder	21	סוּלַּם חֲבָלִים
rowboat	16	סִירַת מְשׁוֹטִים
rubber band	13	גּוּמִיָּיה
rubber stamp	13	חוֹתֶמֶת גּוּמִי
rug	1	שָׁטִיחַ
ruler	1	סַרְגֵּל
run	27	לָרוּץ
running	18	רִיצָה
runway	17	מַסְלוּל
saber-toothed tiger	24	נָמֵר אֲרֹךְ-נִיבִים
sad	26	עָצוּב
saddle	25	אוּכָּף
safe	13	חֲדַר כַּסָּפוֹת
safety deposit box	13	כַּסֶּפֶת
safety net	21	רֶשֶׁת בִּיטָּחוֹן
sail	16	מִפְרָשׂ
sailboat	16	מִפְרָשִׂית
sailing	18	הַפְלָגָה
sailor	15	יַמַּאי
salad	10	סָלָט
salesman	15	אִישׁ מְכִירוֹת
saleswoman	15	מוֹכֶרֶת
salt	10	מֶלַח
sand	22	חוֹל
sandals	7	סַנְדָּלִים
sandbox	8	אַרְגַּז חוֹל
sandpaper	3	נְיַיר לֶטֶשׁ
sandwich	10	כָּרִיךְ
satellite	23	לַוְויָין
saucer	10	תַּחְתִּית
sausages	10	נַקְנִיקִיּוֹת
saw	3	מַסּוֹר
saxophone	19	סַקְסוֹפוֹן
scale	13, 6	מֹאזְנַיִים
scales	22	קַשְׂקַשִּׂים
scarf	7	צָעִיף
scenery	19	תַּפְאוּרָה
school (of fish)	22	לַהֲקַת דָּגִים
school	8	בֵּית-סֵפֶר
school bus	16	אוֹטוֹבּוּס יְלָדִים
scientist	23	מַדְּעָן
scissors	12, 1	מִסְפָּרַיִים
scooter	16	קוֹרְקִינֶט
screw	3	בּוֹרֶג
screwdriver	3	מַבְרֵג
script	19	תַּסְרִיט
scuba diver	22	צוֹלְלָן
sea	32	יָם
sea horse	22	סוּסוֹן יָם
sea turtle	22	צַב יָם
sea urchin	22	קִיפּוֹד יָם
seal	20	כֶּלֶב יָם
seashell	22	קוֹנְכִיָּיה
seat	17	מוֹשָׁב
seat belt	14	חֲגוֹרַת בְּטִיחוּת
seaweed	22	אַצָּה
second	31	שֵׁנִי
secretary	15	מַזְכִּירָה
security camera	13	מַצְלֵמַת בִּיטָּחוֹן
security guard	13	אִישׁ בִּיטָּחוֹן
seesaw	8	עֲלֵה וָרֵד
sell	27	לִמְכּוֹר
seven	31	שֶׁבַע
seventeen	31	שְׁבַע-עֶשְׂרֵה
seventh	31	שְׁבִיעִי

seventy	31	שִׁבְעִים
seventy-eight	31	שִׁבְעִים וּשְׁמוֹנֶה
seventy-five	31	שִׁבְעִים וְחָמֵשׁ
seventy-four	31	שִׁבְעִים וְאַרְבַּע
seventy-nine	31	שִׁבְעִים וְתֵשַׁע
seventy-one	31	שִׁבְעִים וְאַחַת
seventy-seven	31	שִׁבְעִים וְשֶׁבַע
seventy-six	31	שִׁבְעִים וָשֵׁשׁ
seventy-three	31	שִׁבְעִים וְשָׁלוֹשׁ
seventy-two	31	שִׁבְעִים וּשְׁתַּיִים
sewing machine	19	מְכוֹנַת תְּפִירָה
shadow	9	צֵל
shampoo	12	שַׁמְפּוּ
shark	22	כָּרִישׁ
sharp	26	חַד
shaving cream	12	קֶצֶף גִּילּוּחַ
sheep	9	כִּבְשָׂה
sheet	2	סָדִין
sheet music	19	דַּפֵּי תָּוִים
shelf	2	מַדָּף
shield	25	מָגֵן
shipwreck	22	אֳנִיָּיה טְרוּפָה
shirt	7	חוּלְצָה
shoelace	7	שְׂרוֹךְ נַעַל
shoes	7	נַעֲלַיִים
shopping bag	6	שַׂקִּית
shopping cart	6	עֶגְלַת קְנִיּוֹת
short	26, 12	קָצָר
short	26	נָמוּךְ
shorts	7	מִכְנָסַיִים קְצָרִים
shoulder	11	כָּתֵף
shovel	5	אֵת
shower	2	מִקְלַחַת
sidewalk	16	מִדְרָכָה
sign	8, 6	שֶׁלֶט
signature	13	חֲתִימָה
silver	28, 22	כֶּסֶף
sing	27	לָשִׁיר
singer	19	זַמָּר
sink	3	כִּיּוֹר
sister	29	אָחוֹת
sit down	27	לְהִתְיַישֵּׁב
six	31	שֵׁשׁ
sixteen	31	שֵׁשׁ-עֶשְׂרֵה
sixth	31	שִׁישִּׁי
sixty	31	שִׁישִּׁים
sixty-eight	31	שִׁישִּׁים וּשְׁמוֹנֶה
sixty-five	31	שִׁישִּׁים וְחָמֵשׁ
sixty-four	31	שִׁישִּׁים וְאַרְבַּע
sixty-nine	31	שִׁישִּׁים וְתֵשַׁע
sixty-one	31	שִׁישִּׁים וְאַחַת
sixty-seven	31	שִׁישִּׁים וְשֶׁבַע
sixty-six	31	שִׁישִּׁים וָשֵׁשׁ
sixty-three	31	שִׁישִּׁים וְשָׁלוֹשׁ
sixty-two	31	שִׁישִּׁים וּשְׁתַּיִים
skate	27	לְהַחֲלִיק
skateboard	16	סְקֶטְבּוֹרְד
skates	18	מַחֲלִיקַיִים
skating	18	הַחְלָקָה
skeleton	24	שֶׁלֶד
ski	27	לִגְלוֹשׁ
skirt	7	חֲצָאִית
skis	18	מִגְלָשַׁיִים
sky	9	שָׁמַיִם
skydiving	18	צְנִיחָה חוֹפְשִׁית
skyscraper	8	גּוֹרֵד שְׁחָקִים
sled	5	מִזְחֶלֶת
sleep	27	לִישׁוֹן
sleeping bag	9	שַׂק שֵׁינָה
sleeve	7	שַׁרְווּל
slide	8	מַגְלֵשָׁה
sling	11	מַתְלֶה
slow	26	אִיטִּי
small	26	קָטָן
smile	11	חִיּוּךְ
smoke	9	עָשָׁן
smokestack	8	אֲרוּבָּה
snack bar	17	מִזְנוֹן
snake	20	נָחָשׁ
sneeze	11	עִיטּוּשׁ
snorkel	22	שְׁנוֹרְקֶל
snow	5	שֶׁלֶג
snowball	5	כַּדּוּר שֶׁלֶג
snowflake	5	פְּתוֹת שֶׁלֶג
snowman	5	אִישׁ שֶׁלֶג
snowmobile	5	אוֹפַנּוֹעַ שֶׁלֶג
snowplow	5	מְפַלֶּסֶת שֶׁלֶג
snowstorm	5	סוּפַת שֶׁלֶג
soap	6	סַבּוֹן
soccer	18	כַּדּוּרֶגֶל
soccer ball	18	כַּדּוּרֶגֶל
socks	7	גַּרְבַּיִים
sofa	2	סַפָּה
soft	26	רַךְ
soft drink	10	מַשְׁקֶה קַל
solar panel	23	לוּחַ סוֹלָרִי
solar system	23	מַעֲרֶכֶת שֶׁמֶשׁ
somersault	21	סַלְטָה
son	29	בֵּן
soup	10	מָרָק
south	32	דָּרוֹם
South America	32	דְּרוֹם אֲמֶרִיקָה
South Pole	32	הַקּוֹטֶב הַדְּרוֹמִי
southeast	32	דְּרוֹם מִזְרָח
southwest	32	דְּרוֹם מַעֲרָב
space helmet	23	קַסְדַּת חָלָל
space shuttle	23	מַעְבּוֹרֶת חָלָל
space station	23	תַּחֲנַת חָלָל
space suit	23	חֲלִיפַת חָלָל
space walk	23	הֲלִיכָה בֶּחָלָל
spaceship	23	חֲלָלִית
spatula	3	מָרִית
spear	24	חֲנִית
sphere	30	כַּדּוּר
spider	25	עַכָּבִישׁ
spiderweb	25	קוּרֵי עַכָּבִישׁ
spinach	6	תֶּרֶד
spinning wheel	4	גַּלְגַּל טְווִיָּיה
spokes	14	חִישּׁוּרִים
sponge	3	סְפוֹג
spoon	10	כַּף
spotlight	19	זַרְקוֹר
spots	20	חֲבַרְבּוּרוֹת
Spring	5	אָבִיב
sprinkler	5	מַמְטֵרָה
square	8	כִּיכָּר
square	30	רִיבּוּעַ
squid	22	דְּיוֹנוֹן
squire	25	בֶּן לְוָויָה
stable	25	אוּרְווָה
stage	19	בָּמָה
stairs	2	מַדְרֵגוֹת
stamp	13	בּוּל
stand up	27	לַעֲמוֹד
stapler	1	מַכְלֵב
staples	1	סִיכּוֹת
starfish	22	כּוֹכַב יָם
stars	23	כּוֹכָבִים
statue	8	פֶּסֶל
steak	10	אוּמְצָה
steering wheel	14	הֶגֶה
stem	5	גִּבְעוֹל
stethoscope	11	מַסְכֶּת
stick	24	מַקֵּל
stilts	21	קַבַּיִים
stingray	22	טְרִיגוֹן קוֹצָנִי
stirrup	25	אַרְכּוֹף
stop sign	16	תַּמְרוּר עֲצוֹר
stop!	16	עֲמוֹד!
stove	3	כִּירַיִים
straight	12	חָלָק
straw	10	קַשִּׁית
strawberries	6	תּוּתִים
street	16	כְּבִישׁ
string	13, 4	חוּט
strings	19	מֵיתָרִים
stripes	20	פַּסִּים
stroller	16	עֶגְלַת טִיּוּל
student (female)	1	תַּלְמִידָה
student (male)	1	תַּלְמִיד
submarine	22	צוֹלֶלֶת
suds	12	קֶצֶף
sugar	10	סוּכָּר
suit	7	חֲלִיפָה
suitcase	17	מִזְוָודָה
Summer	5	קַיִץ
sun	23	שֶׁמֶשׁ
sunglasses	7	מִשְׁקְפֵי שֶׁמֶשׁ
sunroof	14	גַּג נִפְתָּח
swan	20	בַּרְבּוּר
sweater	7	סְוֶודֶר
sweatpants	7	מִכְנְסֵי טְרֶנִינְג
sweatshirt	7	מֵיזָע
swim	27	לִשְׂחוֹת
swimming	18	שְׂחִיָּיה
swimming pool	18	בְּרֵכַת שְׂחִיָּיה
swings	8	נַדְנֵדוֹת
sword	25	חֶרֶב
swordfish	22	דַּג הַחֶרֶב
t-shirt	7	חוּלְצַת טְרִיקוֹ
table	3	שׁוּלְחָן
table tennis	18	טֶנִיס שׁוּלְחָן
tablecloth	10	מַפַּת שׁוּלְחָן
tail	20	זָנָב
tailor	15	חַיָּט
take a bath	27	לְהִתְרַחֵץ
talk	27	לְדַבֵּר
tall	26	גָּבוֹהַ